Travel Guide to Other Dimensions

with a neurotheological insight into
altered and expanded states of consciousness

Jeanette Woldman, Ph.D.

www.jeanettewoldman.com

www.jeanettewoldman.com

ISBN 978-0-9845310-0-4

Coverdesign by Sha'nah www.shanah.net & ERICKH www.erickh.com.
Cover art "Angel Flight" reprinted with permission from Sha'nah.

For Eric, my mate & best friend in this dimension.

TABLE OF CONTENTS

INTRODUCTION

Most of the planet's peoples believe in a Supreme Being, in non-physical (intelligent) entities, and in other dimensions of reality (ODR) of some sort. Traditionally, encounters with any of these are accomplished by culturally or religiously induced rituals which are performed by select individuals undergoing an altered or expanded state of consciousness (AESC).

For over forty millennia other-worldly beings and non-physical realities have been part of human culture. Cave and rock art around the world from different time periods of different cultures often depict shaman's travels during induced or spontaneous AESC. These voyages express the ODRs the shaman's travels to, and at times depict alien (intelligent) entities he meets under way. The AESC and subsequent journeys of shamans were made possible through different travel-methods, such as for example: psychedelic plant consumption, dreams, out of body experiences, rhythm and dance induced trance.

In today's world, with information at hand through various means of fast data-gathering, and raw materials obtainable from any corner of the world, anyone can attempt to duplicate these otherworldly voyages in a non-traditional, non-religious setting.

Laboratory experiences with volunteers taking psychedelics have shown these to have very much the same experiences during AESC as the shamans during the past millennia. Equally, similar voyages to ODRs and similar encounters with alien intelligent beings are described by (non-shamanic) persons undergoing AESC *outside* a laboratory setting.

We can all undergo altered states, travel to different dimensions, and interact with other (intelligent) entities and maybe even beam home to meet The Divine. And if we do it right, with the proper preparation, we may have a voyage of a lifetime that changes our perspective on classical earthly beliefs forever.

Researcher and journalist Graham Hancock queries whether aliens and UFOs are a brain fiction or in some way real. He questions, that if they are not real, why a minority of every population, running in the tens of millions world wide, make this stuff up? He argues that because huge numbers of people over millennia from different cultures keep on experiencing similar altered states, other realities and other entities, science should stop dismissing and discounting these experiences, and instead seek out a proper explanation.[1]

Modern, Newtonian-based science provides little to no research regarding the validity of these AESC induced travels to ODRs, however, there seems to be an accepted notion that *AESC is required* in order to experience dimensions or entities beyond the earth plane.

Everything we believe is at first constructed by and in our brain. While performing brain scans of persons undergoing AESC we can identify which parts of the brain are activated when dreaming, during trance states, meditation, prayer or under LSD.[2] Certain brain regions apparently play a role in experiencing different ODRs.

Changing the electrochemical and/or the electromagnetic setting of the brain may result in AESC. These altered states may or may not result in visits to other dimensions of reality and/or encounters with alien (intelligent) entities. Because neural activity is electrochemical and brain waves are electromagnetic, brain functions can be modified by altering this environment through use of psychedelics; meditation or prayer; regression hypnosis; resonant entrainment techniques such as binaural beat stimulation; repetitive and rhythmic stimulation; electromagnetic manipulation, etc.

While the physical body of a person undergoing AESC remains

earthbound, it is the person's consciousness (or soul) that enjoys the travel journey. Because the person remains in an awakened state during AESC, he or she is able to recall details of the journey into ODRs.

Actually, there are more similarities and consistencies of account among those who have witnessed ODRs during AESC, as there are when earthly events are witnessed by several people (such as a traffic accident). This may be possible, because these ODRs during altered states are perceived as intensely real. Persons having had these experiences discount the suggestion that these are mainly hallucinations occurring inside their brain. Each and every one of them describe these experiences as profound, real and at times life-altering because of the strong connection with other life forms, the universe or The Divine. Modern science often discarded these notions and experiences, as there exist supposedly no other realities than our earth-bound dimension. Any supernatural experiences are mostly classified as hallucinations or psychosis. Scientific research has a hard time accepting that there may be obtainable knowledge *not* based on our five senses.

Even though modern science many not be ready yet to perform research into ODRs, it has nevertheless opened a way for a few researchers to investigate biological processes in relationships to AESC. These processes in themselves do not give any information about a Supreme Being or about ODRs, but they do break a longstanding taboo and open the way for more in-depth research.

Research into the related neurological components involved by the various AESC's achieved, is wrapped in a novel science called "neurotheology." The term was first coined by writer Aldeus Huxley in his 1962 book "Island". The word is derived from a combination of the pre-fix neuro and the term theology. "Neuro" is a frequently used pre-fix in words related to the brain. Theology is the study of religion, spirituality and God(s) and is derived from the Greek words "theos" (God) and "logia" (words, sayings, discourse). Neurotheology investigates a (biological) basis in the brain for spiritual experience, for altered states of consciousness, and for other dimensions of reality.

Andrew Newberg, M.D. is an associate professor of Radiology and Psychiatry and an adjunct assistant professor of Religious Studies at the University of Pennsylvania. He is also director of the Center for Spirituality and the Mind. He conducts neurological research related to spiritual experiences: "..it is imperative that one recognizes that taking a brain image of someone having a spiritual experience may not help determine the ultimate causal basis of such an experience. One conclusion is that the experience is, in fact, nothing more then a series or conglomeration of brain functions. This would relegate religion and its theological development to a human construction. Another conclusion would be that the brain is truly in contact with some divine presence or fundamental level of reality. In this case, the brain scan images are merely detecting the effect of that reality on the human brain. In this regard, religious experience does, in fact, coincide with a higher level of reality that transcends our usual experience of the material world. There is a third conclusion that is possible, which in some sense, is a synthesis of the first two. In such a conclusion, the answer to one of the commonly posed questions, "Did God create the brain or did the brain create God? would be "yes" to both."[3]

Some of the information pertaining to this book is based on classical Newtonian science. However, other information falls outside the realm and definition of the current scientific method; the so-called post-modern science. This information obtained through post-modern science will nevertheless be treated seriously, as the limited scope of the current classic scientific process should not limit the scope and arguments set forth in this book.

This Travel Guide discusses different AESC methods, their related ODRs and subsequent brain-activity. The AESC methods to travel to ODRs are:

- Psychedelics
- Meditation and prayer
- Regression hypnosis
- Binaural beat stimulation
- Repetitive and rhythmic stimulation
- Electric and electromagnetic stimulation
- Disease
- Deprivation of essential elements
- Magnetic field disturbances
- UFO Abductions

PART I

BACKGROUND BASICS

Consciousness, the Body, and Altered States

Consciousness & Subconsciousness

Consciousness is defined in this book as:

1. Having an awareness of one's environment and one's own existence, sensations, and thoughts. In addition to this definition, consciousness will include (lucid) awareness during meditative, dreaming, sleeping and altered states.

2. Being our ultimate essence or energy-force that lives forever and is immortal. Consciousness can also be referred to as "soul" or "pure consciousness" or "non-physical body" or "unique self-aware ethereal energy".

3. Consciousness is that part of us that travels during AESC.

4. Consciousness is often explained by other non-earthly intelligent beings as levels of vibration. The higher one's consciousness development, the higher one vibrates, and the less physical the person becomes. The cycle of death and reincarnation (for consciousness development) will be stopped once the desired consciousness-level (and thus vibrational rate) has been achieved. There will then be no more return into the physical realm, but further evolution continues in a spiritual realm.[1]

Consciousness is not to be confused with "self" or "ego". The ego is an assemblage of experiences, memories and emotions gathered and attained by a person. Consciousness exists before, after, and during the lifetime of a person. The ego exists only during the time span of a person's lifetime.

Subconsciousness (or unconsciousness) will be defined as the

9

part of the psyche lying far below consciousness which is not easily raised into consciousness.[2] It will also be defined as the state in which mental processes take place without the conscious perception of the individual. The subconscious contains elements of psychic makeup, such as memories or repressed desires and traumas that are not subject to conscious perception or control, but often affect conscious thoughts and behavior. The subconscious may also attain memories of previous lives and of life after death. The subconscious can be consciously accessed during AESC. In this book unconsciousness is considered the same as subconsciousness.

Consciousness & the Body

Robert Monroe is an "out-of-body-travel" expert and the (diseased) founder of the Monroe Institute, whereby through means of binaural beat stimulation with (non) audible frequencies persons undergo AESC and visit ODRs. He explained to his research volunteer Rosalind A. McKnight that "the physical body is an illusion here when you're born, and gone when you die."[3] And through information obtained from alien intelligent beings McKnight learned that death is just a change in vibrational rate onward to a new existence, since a true OBE is not a movement through space, but a change in vibration from the denser physical self to the higher vibration of the etheric self.[4]

She was informed that if we would be taught *how* to think, instead of *what* to think, our mind could travel anywhere in the universe, and tap into all knowledge that is there. The basic form of communication, our mind, is by design already on a wavelength of very high vibration.[5]

Evolution passes through the mineral, vegetable and animal kingdom. A group soul of animals can evolve into human consciousness. Earth is a tough place to be, and the reason for spiritual growth. Soul development is combined with vibrations at higher and faster rate. Helping others is essential

10

for progress. The higher a soul vibrates, the more responsibilities it has.[6]

Robert Monroe writes that he, and thousands of participants that have gone through the programs at the Monroe Institute, were explained by alien entities that our "souls" are a form of energy that enters our physical body prior to birth, and leaves it after death, with as aim to become more educated. This energy can take various forms. He defines human consciousness as non-physical and non-time-space-dependent, and a manifestation of this energy. Earth presents an intense learning process for this energy, but has certain rules of engagement, such as: acceptance of time-space existence; sublimation of previous physical experiences; a purpose or a goal to obtain; selection of entry-point into the physical body; learning to live with five senses, conscious awareness, emotions, ego; releasing value judgments; detachments of matter and persons; enjoying laughter; going through a pain and pleasure learning curve. This information is very similar to those obtained from persons undergoing (spiritual) regression hypnosis.[7] Monroe states that fear is the great obstacle to human growth.[8]

State of consciousness	Explanation
Waking	Only state which is perceived in consciousness.
Dreaming	Less conscious state, commencing unconscious state. However with growth and development consciousness can enter the dream state, called lucid dreaming.
Sleeping	Ultimate state of unconsciousness, however with training one can remain conscious while in the sleep state during deep meditation.
"AESC" Altered or Expanded States of Consciousness	Dreaming and sleeping state while remaining conscious, such as meditative states, trance, hypnotic/hypnagogic states, out of body states (OBE), near death experiences (NDE), and lucid dreaming. There are four levels to define.
Light AESC ⟱	Consciousness and subconsciousness apparently coincide somewhere between 6.8 and 8.3 Hz
	This is a state of "mind awake, body asleep"[a]

Medium AESC ↓	"Expanded awareness"[b] Leaving behind the physical body and experiencing the etheric body. In the mood to head out and explore. Often accompanied with fear, therefore in OBE, souls often fold back into their bodies. One may have the feeling of flying. Rosalind A. McKnight states that sexual energy may be strong at this point.[c] Possibility of encountering intelligent beings, some of which seem to help their human counterpart to get through the human experience. Some claim to assist transition to other dimensions. Some assist humans to obtain OBE by helping to lift them out of their physical body. Trust and "letting go of fear" are essential to explore Focus levels from here onward.
	According to Rosalind A. this is the state of "no time" whereby 3 hours seems like 2 minutes. McKnight states that this is the emotional level of the self, leaving behind both the physical and etheric body.[d] At this level the soul experiences direct confrontations and meetings with loved ones, and can relive energies from past lives (similar as some experiences in the Ultimate Reality). Earth is ideal for emotional growth of a soul.
Deep AESC	Complete of the physical, etheric and mental body. Moving to a variety of ODRs. Bridge into worlds with non-human entities (similar to the Humanoid ODR). Equivalent to deep (delta) sleep with the mind fully awake. The edge between time-space and non physical energy.
State of Pure Consciousness In this book also referred to as "pure consciousness"	Ultimate AESC: altered states beyond those described above are equivalent to identification or union with something larger then the self or The Divine (see definition of God and The Divine further below). Also referred to as a Mystical State, such as Enlightenment (Buddhism) or a State of Oneness with The Divine or Unio Mystica (non Buddhism). The self, time, space and physical sensations seem to dissipate in this state. Mind and matter become one. To obtain this elevated state, one is to quiet the awakened mind, set fears aside and free consciousness from the ego.

Table 1 – Consciousness States

ODRs (Other Dimensions of Reality)

Where To and How Far?

To put things a little bit into perspective regarding the dimension called "our universe":

- Our solar system is located in the Milky Way galaxy. The Milky Way holds billions of stars. The universe itself holds billions of galaxies.

- To get an idea of distance, imagine you could travel with the speed of light (nearly 300 Km/sec). It would take you a good second to reach the moon, approximately 6-8 minutes to reach the sun (since we go around the sun in an elliptically, the speed depends on the earth's distance away from the sun). To go to the closest star in our galaxy would take 4 years. To go to the nearest neighboring galaxy would take over 2.2 million years.

- To get into the matter of scale; the largest known star to date is VY Canis Majoris, located some 4900 light years away from us. This star is about 2000 times larger than the sun. Earth would fit 7 quadrillion times into VY Canis Majoris.[1]

- And something about energy output: Quasars are distant galaxies with a tremendous energy output, located between some 780 million and 28 billion light years away. The first quasar to be identified is 3C 273, located at 33 light years away with a luminosity of about two trillion times that of our sun.[2]

Despite the above facts about distance and space of the universe, we are nevertheless able to access ODRs almost instantaneously. While our physical bodies remain earthbound, (part of) our consciousness travels elsewhere. Some visits may last several minutes, while others may last many hours. Because time and space do not exist during AESC and to where we travel to, we loose notion of it when en-route.

Psychiatrist and past-life regression therapist Brian Weiss' quotes from his patients under hypnosis: "When I talk about other dimensions, I mean other energetic states or even different levels of consciousness, not necessarily other planetary systems or galaxies."[3] "Earth, the three-dimensional world, is not really our true home."[4] "There are many worlds and dimensions...many, many more souls than there are physical containers."[5] "As the vibrational energy of spirits is slowed down so that more dense environments such as your three-dimensional plane [referring to earth] can be experienced, the effect is for spirit to be crystallized and transformed into denser and denser bodies. The densest of all is the physical state. The vibrational rate is the slowest. Time appears faster in this state because it is inversely related to the vibrational rate. As the vibrational rate is increased, time slows down. This is how there can be difficulty in choosing the right body, the right time of re-entry into the physical state."[6] Psychiatrist Brian Weiss M.D. uses past-life regression therapy to heal current life traumas and illnesses. Weiss is a graduate of Columbia University and Yale Medical School, and the former Chairman of Psychiatry at the Mount Sinai Medical Centre in Miami. He practices in Miami, Florida.

Rosalind A. McKnight writes: "Within the human form are billions of universes that have within them universes. The universe that man can see through the microscope and telescope is the universe on the same vibration as the universe that makes up the particles of the body. Each galaxy is only a cluster of atoms operating on the same vibration...There is no other reality than true *being*...There is only one reality and that is the God-force, as you call it. All else is an illusion."[7]

So where do we go, and who or what do we encounter? Apparently the ODRs we travel to are related to the obtained means and methods of the various AESC. Who and what we encounter seems in turn related to the ODR we travel to.

The ultimate encounter most travelers aim to have is with The Divine, the purest and most loving consciousness of which we are all part of, and which is ever present in a dimension called the Ultimate Reality.

Unpleasant encounters do occur, but are rare for the well-prepared and well-informed traveler. In some events, even the well-seasoned traveler may undergo an unlikable, or at times painful, encounter with an alien being. However, most of these unpleasant encounters seem a trade-off against important information provided (pain, but gain). Almost all non-earthly beings with which the traveler interacts are intelligent, well meaning, helpful, and provide useful information.

What is The Divine?
Interviewer: "Do you believe in God?"
Respondent: "Yes."
Interviewer: "Do you believe in a God who can change the course of events on earth?"
Respondent: "No, just the ordinary one." [8]

In this book, the contemporary word "God" will be frequently listed as "The Divine" and will be identified with "the ultimate, positive, loving, peaceful, and compassionate creator energy of all that exists and of which we are part of". The Divine does not require ritual, rules, regulations, sacrifice or behavioral codes.

Robert Monroe describes The Divine, our Creator as: "..the designer of the ongoing process of which we are a part...does not demand worship, adoration, or recognition...does not punish for evil and misdeeds...does not intercede or interdict in our life activity...does not punish for our "evil" and "misdeeds"...does not intercede or interdict in our life activity."[9] Information received through Monroe Institute participants confirms the existence of The Divine, as a loving, creative, high conscious energy. It is emphasized that we (our non-physical "we") are part of this source.

Rosalind A. McKnight was one of the foremost "test persons" at the early stages of the Monroe Institute. During AESC at the Institute, God, The Divine, was described to her by alien intelligent beings as follows: "Man was created in the likeliness of God; therefore, man is God. And the man who separates himself from the true God-self is an adherent to the earth religion, which is man-made and falls short of the true reality of the higher God-Self...God is that vital living force in all that is real...The force that is pure love and pure energy is what man would label God."[10] According to McKnight's informers, the highest known energy is love, which one must have completely for one self before one can share love with others.[11]

Religion	Names for The Divine in various religions
Judaism	Elohim, YHVH, YHWH
Christianity	God, Yahweh, Jehovah, Deus, I AM
Islam, Bahá'i Faith	Allah, Mighty, the All-Powerful, the Merciful, the Ever-Forgiving, the Omniscient
Rastafari	Jah
Chinese religions	Shang Ti, Shen, Zu, Tian Zu, Tian
Hinduism	Brahman, Vishnu, Shiva, Krishna
Ayyavazhi	Ekam
Sikhism	Allah, Raam, Hari, Akal Purakh, Ek Onkar
Zoroastrianism	Ahura Mazda
Other words for **The Divine**	The Source, Love, Pure Consciousness, Cosmic Consciousness, Lord, Father, Supreme Being, Maker, Deity, Pure Mind, Almighty, Devine, Spirit, Creator, Big Mind, Absolute Unitary Being, Tao, Ein Sof, All Knowing Presence, Oversoul, Oneness

Table 2 – The Divine

What is Real?

What is real and what is perceived as real may or may not be one and the same. Scientific or objective reality is based on the belief that nothing is more real than the material world. This in contrast to mystics, who believe they can experience a primary reality that runs deeper than material existence. What we think of as reality is only a rendition of reality that is created by the brain.[12]

Various researchers write clear statements about our perceived reality and about our direct environment. Andrew Newberg & Eugene d'Aguilli: "Nothing enters consciousness whole. There is no direct, objective experience of reality."[13] The late Eugene d'Aquili M.D., Ph.D., was a clinical assistant professor in the Department of Psychiatry at the University of Pennsylvania (✝ 1998).

Andrew Newberg and Robert Waldman: "..everything we see is an illusion, in the sense that our eyes, memories, and consciousness can envision only a symbolic representation of the world."[14] "Most people find it difficult to accept the notion that the reality we perceive is not exactly the reality existing "out there", but a thorough review of the literature on perception suggests that we do not need a precise or complete representation of any object, face, or scene in order to maintain a stable impression of the world."[15] Waldman is a therapist and an Associate Fellow at the Center for Spirituality and the Mind, University of Pennsylvania

Research writer with a BA in Philosophy, Matthew Alper: "Every culture – no matter how isolated - has perceived reality as consisting of two distinct realms: the physical and the spiritual."[16]

Research writer Laurence O. McKinney: "Reality is not decreed, it is perceived."[17]

Psychedelics expert Timothy Leary: "We translated the basic Hindu teaching that everything is an illusion into the modern neurological truth that *everything is a figment of your own brain.*"[18]

Rosalind A. McKnight writes that reality is often confused in our physical state, as there exist no physical state but a pure energy state of consciousness.[19] "The earth is here, but is not here...It exists only for those who experience it as existing...Because we experience the physical earth, feel the physical body around our being, and observe the other planets and galaxies through telescopes, does not mean this is the reality of existence. It is not. It is only a temporary energy manifestation of the real, which exists strictly within the internal nature of the self...The physical earth is an emotional level for those souls who need this type of physical manifestation for emotional cleansing and growth."[20]

Earth, ODRs and Encounters

Earth is our material reality, our current-day world as perceived by our senses during our waking state. Robert Monroe, describes the world in which we live as Locale I.[21]

Rosalind A. McKnight received information from non-earthly intelligent beings that a person's vibratory level is unique, just as a fingerprint, and that each soul has its own soul-print. The non-earthly dimension has no time and space and has a higher level of vibration then earth. Earth has one of the lowest-vibrating energies.[22]

Earth is explained to McKnight as only a reflection of the "real world", and in a state of (consciousness) imbalance, due to the ego-power struggle. Only pure love creates overall oneness and balance. Natural disasters are the result of the imbalance of earth-consciousness, which is directly related to its inhabitants which make up the physical part of it.[23] War is explained as a manifestation of fear.[24]

McKnight was informed about dualism that it exists only outside the nature of The Divine (The Divine is oneness) on our physical plane. Only when we realize The Divine on earth, we can turn our energies into purity and perfection, which is oneness. "Ego" is part or our dual thinking, and only exists in the earth reality.[25]

Terence McKenna states that the physics of light is an alternative physics, since light being composed of photons it has no antiparticle, and no dualism in its world.[26]

ODR (other dimensions of reality) are other worldly, non-material and non-physical dimensions of reality as perceived by persons during AESC. During AESC the earth reality disintegrates and seemingly transforms persons, objects, and self to enter gradually into an ODR. Various ODRs can be experienced at the same time, and transition from one to another is not always evident. For centuries and still today, ODR has been called the "spirit world" by shamans.

Persons visiting ODRs describe the experience as "more real then real" and these visits often have a life-changing impact. Whereas earthly experiences may fade with time, ODR experiences seem to be vividly remembered.

Earth and Various ODRs in general categories (in random order)	
Earth	Our material world as perceived in our waking state. Referred to as "Locale I" by the Monroe Institute.
Shadow ODR	Realities which are perceived as less positive and less loving. During AESC this reality may be *perceived* because the traveler has not been able to let go of his/her fears, and/or has not made the proper preparations. This is part of Locale II, with motion and matter, according to the Monroe Institute. It may contain similarities to "hell" (which in turn may or may not be attributes of our own egos).
Geometric ODR	Realities in which (colorful) motives, icons and patterns with an abstract and/or geometric and/or DNA theme are predominant. Apparently one passes this dimension prior to all others.
Hybrid ODR	Realities in which alien (intelligent) beings such as beasts, human/animal hybrids, human/insect hybrids, therianthropes (part man/part beast), chimeras, monsters, reptiles, snakes, insects, theatrical figures, figures with masks and clown like entities exist. The person undergoing AESC may transform into one of these entities.

Earth and Various ODRs in general categories (in random order), continued	
Humanoid ODR	Realities where advanced humanoid intelligences exist, who are often described as having a domed triangulated head with insect like eyes, or looking like elves, fairies or trolls.
Earthlike ODR	Realities which has the same look and feel as earth, except that times and places seem distorted or out of place. This is another part of what the Monroe Institute calls Locale II. They state this to be the natural environment of our non-physical bodies and is inhabited by a variety of entities. It seems also to describe part of Locale III, which is earthlike without past or present.
Ultimate Reality	A reality where only loving entities live. This reality is our (soul's) actual home base and our original source of existence and consciousness. It is also referred to as Other Side, Heaven, Home and Higher Level of Consciousness.

Table 3 – Earth and ODRs

Shadow ODR

The Shadow ODR is described by hypnotized subjects as the temporary world visited after our passing prior to accessing the Ultimate Reality and/or the temporary world visited between our reincarnations, comparable to the Tibetan Bardo world. Brian Weis writes about near death experiences and the Shadow ODR: "When you find the light, you find peace, comfort and love. There is nothing negative about such a beautiful experience. I have never found hell, only different levels of ignorance. The more ignorance, the less light."[27]

Dr. Michael Newton writes that he has never encountered a subject speaking of hell. Apparently, when a soul has done evil acts on earth, the soul will enter an area in heaven (The Ultimate Reality) where "their energy will be remodeled to make it whole again".[28] It should be noted that this is not considered punishment. However, souls who have committed suicide with a healthy body apparently have a reckoning according to Michael Newton, as it is a sudden development stop that has to be re-lived on earth soonest thereafter. Michael Newton's research encompasses four decades worth of hypnotherapy and regression therapy whereby the state of lives between reincarnations is recalled. Michael Duff Newton holds a doctorate in Counseling Psychology and is a certified Master Hypnotherapist. He holds private practice in Lost Angeles and has been on the faculty of several higher educational institutions. He is also a lecturer.

Psychic and hypnotherapist Sylvia Browne speaks of "The Dark Side" when referring the Shadow ODR.[29] She describes this to be an area where those souls go after death who have not accepted the light of the Ultimate Reality. They recycle between earth in the Shadow ODR until they return eventually to the Ultimate Reality. Also Sylvia Browne does not speak of punishment. Both Newton and Browne write that some confused souls that return to the Ultimate Reality require special care and will be "deprogrammed" of earthly traumas.

Robert Monroe also encountered unfriendly entities, which he supposes could be reflections of himself, but he cannot be certain about this. At times he felt another body behind him, only to discover that this was indeed himself.[30]

Geometric ODR
The Geometric ODR is a reality in which (colorful) motives, icons and patterns with an abstract and/or geometric theme are predominant. This dimension can be traveled to through various means of obtaining AESC. Also mandala-like figures and fleur-de-lis figures and landscape-like environments are reported. The DNA-double helices occur frequently, spiraling and twirling. Fantasy alphabets, numbers, threads of words and (Mayan, Egyptian) hieroglyphic writing have also been noted. Apparently one passes this dimension previous to reaching others.

Prior to Cro Magnon art, there is evidence of symbolism in the form of geometric patterns on objects found in the Bomblos Cave of South Africa, dating some 77,000 years back, however this is a far predecessor from the full-blown art found in France and Spain some 40 millennia later. Engraved geometric patterns are also found in ancient Australian rock art dating back over 40,000 years ago. Whereas European art stopped around 12,000 years ago, cave art in Africa dates back to just 100 years ago.[31]

From left to right:
- Cro-Magnon cave art in the Castillo Cave, Cantabria, Spain
- Nevada Indian rock art
- Pueblo rock art at Dry Fork Valley, Utah, USA

Hybrid ODR

The Hybrid ODR is a reality in which beasts, human/animal hybrids, human/insect hybrids, therianthropes (part man/part beast), chimeras, monsters, reptiles, snakes, insects, stick-figures, theatrical figures in a circus like environment, figures with masks and clown-like entities exist. Bee-hive type structures are also frequently described. All entities seem intelligent. This dimension can be traveled to through various means of obtaining AESC, however the use of psychedelics and repetitive & rhythmic stimulation seems to provide the most efficient access to this reality. Cave and rock art paintings often depict these so-called therianthropes no matter where in the world these are located. Therianthropic and geometric patterned art and sculpture are also seen in abundance in Mayan art and ancient Egyptian art.

Curling snakes, serpents coiled into double helices and DNA motives are also a frequent recurring description in this reality. At times the person undergoing AESC is transformed

22

into one of these entities. Change-perception in body image and feelings occurs, such as: transformation from stick-like-figures to zigzag figures; extra fingers, legs or arms; shortening of limbs; stretching-sensation of the scalp; prickling of skin; feeling of insects crawling and biting under skin. Pain and abuse may take place, such as: skin-penetration by spears, arrows, darts or other objects; stabbing, piercing and pricking; eating of body parts by other entities; incurred wounds; being stung, bitten or impaled; dismemberment; insertion of sacred stones or rock crystals into the body, but also rape. Some subjects explain that these entities were interested in learning about emotion and feelings.

However, subjects entering this stage claim often to gain knowledge from inhabitants of the reality in exchange for these unpleasant exams. These inhabitants may be referred to as guides or helpers. Encounters with these entities, however painful and traumatic, are therefore nevertheless often perceived as a learning experience.

An example are shamans who return from AESC with the power to heal, make rain, find lost objects or control prey animals after having undergone transformation, pain and dismemberment in the ODR to be reborn when going back to the earth reality (so called surrender to pain and death to obtain knowing power). It is stated by the shamans that during this stage they fully enter their AESC. These so-called supernatural helpers may already appear as an animal or therianthrope when the shaman is a child until initiation. This experience is in parallel to UFO abductees who have been contacted since childhood until abduction. In many other tribal traditions, animals are seen as spirit guides or helper guides.

Piercing or wounding by arrows or other objects of a (naked) person, to henceforth undergo a transition from death to another reality is a common theme of shamans undergoing AESC. This theme is also depicted in Upper Paleolithic cave art (Cave of Pech Merle, Cabrerets; Cave of Cougnac, Payrignac; Cave of Cosquer, Cassis; all in France). It also occurs in religious martyrdom stories, such as those of St. Sebastien, St. Ursula, St. Theresa of Avila and Jesus. Jesus had his hands and feet nailed to the cross and bleed from a pierced wound on his right side (different accounts in different religious writings). St. Sebastian was the target of Roman archers, and then was eventually beaten to death with clubs. He is often depicted naked with multiple arrows. The ecstasy of St. Teresa of Avila depicts her dream by which an angel pierced her heart with an arrow of divine love.

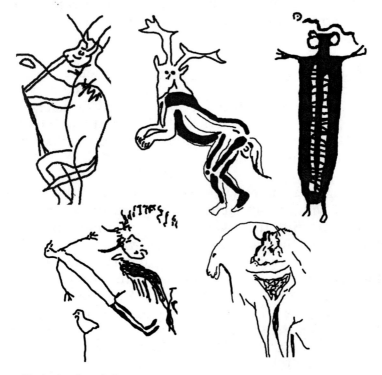

Clockwise from left:
- The "Petit Sourcier" (small shaman or witch). Cro-Magnon cave art of half man-half bison in the Trois Frères cave in Montesquieu-Avantès, in the province of Ariège, South-WestFrance.
- The "Sourcier", also called "Horned God", from the same cave depicts a drawing of a hybrid of various animals and man.
- Part of the "Head of Sinbad" panels. Hopi Indian rock art in the Buckhorn Wash region, San Rafael River, Utah, USA
- Cro-Magnon cave art in the Shaft of the Dead Man, Cave of Lascaux, France.
- Bison/lion heads with female parts called the "Ponte d'Arc Venus" in the cave of Cavault, France

Humanoid ODR

The Humanoid ODR is a reality where advanced humanoid intelligences exist, who are often described as having a domed triangulated head with insect like eyes and a small or no mouth. Also humanoids looking like elves, fairies and trolls are often depicted, as well as UFO objects and UFO contact. Subjects often refer to these entities as android-like or alien beings. This dimension can be traveled to through various means of obtaining AESC, however psychedelic-use and repetitive & rhythmic stimulation seems to provide the most efficient access to this reality. The setting may be in a cave, under water or in a high technology environment with computers and an operating theatre. Sometimes a nursery type setting is described, or a playroom. The extra-terrestrials are shape shifters who can disguise at will their form (animal, human, alien, mermaids, mermen) and appearance (transparent, light-like). Apparently their transportation modes can also change shape, and like themselves, can move through solids, walls and closed windows.

The means of entering this reality through AESC is often described as floating, levitation, flight through air with a beam of light, ropes, string or climbing.

As with the Hybrid ODR (which can blend or merge into this ODR), painful probing, operations and rape in exchange for knowledge seems a possibility to occur here. Operations with probes and crystals, insertion of objects and crystals into body cavities, and extraction of brain and eyes are common descriptions of experiences. Some subjects describe that they had the feeling their DNA was manipulated or changed of structure.

Knowledge may also be transferred by insight in "sacred books".

At times, Robert Monroe encountered friendly intelligent entities that invaded his head, apparently searching every memory in his mind.[32] He writes about recordings of participants undergoing sessions at the Monroe Institute.

These participants were in the OBE state, but clearly conscious and able to record their experience and information they received from other intelligent beings.[33] Apparently characters and situations can be invented, just as with daydreams, except that it is dreamt by a more advanced sort of consciousness.[34]

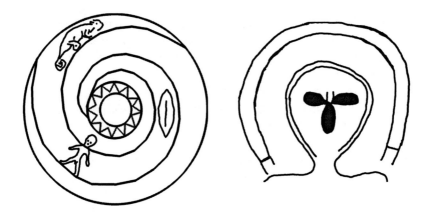

From left to right:
- Nepalese plate dated from 3000 BC (note the reptile, humanoid and UFO on it).
- Ancient Australian rock art paintings of "Vondijna", the mouth-less God of creation.

The various encounters with other intelligent (energy or light) entities, as described by the many volunteers at the Monroe Institute, seem often to gather information on the part of the alien intelligent entities. These beings accessed memories of the volunteers and performed experiments. They are apparently capable of doing so by removing the energy essence of a human (soul), without disturbing the physical body. At times the soul was taken along on expeditions to other realities. It seems that they are able to change matter, but not produce it. The communication form used by the alien beings with Monroe's subjects is always non-verbal, instant and telepathic. No abuse or violence by these seemingly peaceful beings has ever been reported.

Monroe refers to some of the intelligent beings as INSPECS (intelligent species). These in particular always assisted and helped him (and others) when in the OBE state. However they are not the only ones. Also the INSPECS claim that humans are created by the same source, and that the human experience is just temporary. Free will is described as an essential part of this experience. Some of the INSPECS have had a human experience; others used other centers in other universes for consciousness growth.[35] Robert A. Monroe describes visits during OBE states to other realities. These visits were usually guided by an INSPEC. The physical universe and humankind are considered an ongoing creative process for our soul.

While visiting certain alien intelligent beings during one particular session, McKnight describes how she was hooked up to a machine that apparently tapped into her brainwaves, and let her see her own birth process, where she was prior to this birth when she choose this life. Hell is described as a something believers create; it does not exist outside the physical mind; it represents man locked in to his own unreality. McKnight's current life lessons and goals were discussed with other souls (also referred to as groups of souls working together on certain levels or rates of vibration or "group souls"). Her lessons are about patience and acceptance. Prior to coming to the earth dimension, she chose her parents and family situation (four brothers and three sisters) to better accomplish these goals. Because earth energies are much more intense then in other dimensions, and because of its duality and frictions, it is ideal for rapid growth of a soul. Growth comes only with sharing and interchanging energies with other souls.[36] The time on earth is seen as a "projected state", of which each soul writes its own script and plays its own roles and thus acts as an observer of life, and is therefore *not being alive*. We are actors on our soul's stage of reality while living in its pure energy. [37]

McKnight was informed that the cycle of death and rebirth continues as long as we are separated from our own reality. Once we become aware of this, we can look back into our original source. Being aware of one's own reality is true worship, and all forms of man-made religions are therefore not true.[38]

Sexual encounters to produce hybrid offspring is a recurring theme. Energy flow from the genitals or stomach towards the head is also frequently reported. Offspring apparently is described as pale, sickly with white hair and skin. Marriage and loyalty towards the humanoid partner is another recurring theme. However, the humanoid entities are mostly described as emotionless and loveless. It seems they are interested in obtaining our sense of love and affection (hence the interbreeding program).

Monroe also outlines, that when changing from one dimension to another, he was often accompanied by a strong sex drive. To overcome this, he had to set it aside, rather then confront it. He analyses that this sex drive has something to do with the "force" that pushes the non-physical out of the body. He compares this with penile erection that male subjects undergo during REM sleep (rapid eye movement). When Monroe did have "sex" in other Locales, it was described as a merging of two forms reaching "an unbearable ecstasy, and then tranquility, equalization, and it is over."[39] He believes that the sex-drive could be a catalyst to the vibrational condition and a doorway to the Second State.[40]

Encounters with these humanoids, however painful and traumatic, are often perceived as a learning experience (same as with the Hybrid ODR). Rick Strassman quotes a volunteer describing an interaction in the extraterrestrial reality: "They wanted me to look into their bodies. I saw inside them and understood reproduction, what it's like before birth, the passage into the body."[41] All of the above descriptions are very similar to those described by UFO abductees during their voyage. Rick Strassman M.D. conducted from 1990-1995 DEA-approved clinical research on DMT (one of the most powerful psychedelics known). Strassman holds degrees from Stanford University and Albert Einstein College of Medicine of Yeshiva University.

Earthlike ODR
The earthlike ODRs are a variety of transient dimensions that have the same look and feel as earth. These dimensions seem to be easiest traveled through and to through AESC obtained by binaural beat stimulation.

The Monroe Institute identifies several of these dimensions by so-called "Focus Levels". Robert A. Monroe outlines these as follows:

- Focus 22 is a dimension where humans which are still in physical existence, have only partial consciousness, such as those suffering from chemical dependency, dementia, or those who are anesthetized or comatose. Travel to this dimension may be recalled as dreams or hallucinations. It is a place where those with "loose, chaotic thoughts" go after death.
- Focus 23 is a dimension where those souls go after the death, which seem unable to free themselves from earth. In this dimension there is an unawareness of death.
- Focus levels 24 to 26 are dimensions containing belief system territories. These are dimensions where dogmatically inclined souls go after death, due to religious and philosophical beliefs instilled on earth. Souls seem to have an awareness of death, but do not know where they are or where to go, thus remaining in a state of shock; they are waiting to be taken to the next Focus level.
- Focus 27 is a dimension referred to as a way-station. It is a place of high creativity and a stepping stone to areas beyond, such as the Ultimate Reality. It is an artificial place created by human minds to ease transition after our death out of the physical reality. This area holds a "reception center" where loved ones (souls who are no longer in physical bodies) welcome others that have just left their physical bodies on earth. Here they are counseled about their next step.[42]

Ultimate Reality
The Ultimate Reality is a dimension where only loving entities exist. It is also often referred to as "heaven". This reality is our

(soul's) actual home base. This is a place where our etheric substance (our consciousness) goes after our passing for further growth and development of our soul. This dimension is the most sought after reality and can be traveled to through various means of obtaining AESC. Regression hypnosis, binaural beat stimulation and psychedelic-use seem to provide the most efficient access to this reality.

Brian Weiss refers to the Ultimate Reality is "another dimension, a higher level of consciousness or higher state of consciousness".[43] Niels Hendrik Gregersen writes that in the Bible's Matthew, the kingdom of God is also called the kingdom of the heavens, whereby heaven is a symbol of those aspects of creation that are beyond our control, and yet determine our existence.[44]

The Ultimate Reality is associated with abundant feelings of love, joy, peace, tranquility, happiness, timelessness, limitless. Apparently a soul in pure energy state no longer feels hate, anger, envy, jealousy, etc.

Robert Monroe has been able to visit a deceased friend in another dimension, where the friend appeared half a century younger and still performing his "earth" job as doctor, however, Monroe has not found anything that looked or resembled The Divine or an after-life-heaven as described in many books of faith. He did visit a most peaceful place he refers to as "Home". In this reality there is no male, female and no positive or negative. Monroe writes that this dimension can be visited in the OBE state. He describes it as a place with many colors and beautiful music with which one vibrates in harmony.[45] There seems to be a Force or Godlike energy which seems The Divine, but Monroe does not describe this energy fully. Several of Monroe's escapades focus on consulting his Life Book and interacting with it.

Monroe's Focus Level 28 may be the Ultimate Reality, as he describes it as a spiritual area whereby it is rare for a soul in a physical earthbound body to go this far, as it can take the physical body out of its dimension. This gives an explanation for bi-location, or being seen at two places at once. Place beyond time-space and human thought. Limits return to a physical human body.[46]

Researcher Rick Strassman mentions one of his psychedelic DMT-induced volunteers visiting this reality and realizing that all earthly things (family ties, job, plans, and memories) were not important and very remote; as if the Ultimate Reality was the real, and only important reality.[47]

Travel to the Ultimate Reality is often accompanied by high-speed travel through a tunnel accompanied by voices, songs or music and a bright light. Deceased relatives, friends or family may wait at the end of the tunnel. A visit to the Ultimate Reality is always described as "very real" or "more real then real". For most people who have visited this reality, it has been a life altering experience.

Psychic Sylvia Browne describes the surroundings of the Ultimate Reality ("The Other Side in her vocabulary) with a topography similar to the earth, without precipitation, with soft breezes as strongest winds and a constant temperature of 78 degrees Fahrenheit. The Ultimate Reality has almost all earth-animals, except insects. [48] She describes traveling to the Ultimate Reality as follows: "..the deafening crack is a phenomenon called "rapport", which happens when an abrupt sound pierces the "veil" between The Other Side's dimension and ours, much like the sonic boom of the sound barrier being broken."[49] "The Other Side isn't some distant paradise beyond the clouds. It really exists right here among us, only three feet above our ground level, simply in another dimension with a much higher vibration then ours."[50] "..every adult on earth, no matter what their race, nationality, religion, or lack of one, experiences exactly the same tunnel toward exactly the same sacred light of God."[51]

Robert Monroe's OBE's sometimes came with a hissing sound coming from the forebrain. He noticed that scenarios being played following this particular hissing sound often were predictions of future events.[52]

Brian Weiss, Michael Newton and Sylvia Browne quote their hypnotized patients:

- Weiss: "Everything comes from the light. Our soul immediately goes there."[53]
- Newton: "Time has no meaning in the spirit world."[54] "Righteousness, honesty, humor and love are the primary foundations of our life after life."[55]
- Browne: "..there is really no such thing as time in the context of eternity on The Other Side."[56]

The Silver Cord and the Shape of our Soul

Sylvia Browne speaks of a silver cord, very much like an umbilical cord attached to the lower breast bone that connects us with our source and feeds us with life force and love.[57] This silver cord has connotations in many eastern religions and in the yoga tradition.

Robert Monroe's also located a "cord" attached from his physical to his non-physical body, and described it as a two-inch-thick cable. Monroe also found that the non-physical body was subject to gravitational forces, electricity and electro-magnetic energy. The non-physical body is also plastic, able to take on any form desired; at times visible; having a sense of touch; and seemingly a direct reversal of the physical body.[58]

Daily Life at the Ultimate Reality

Michael Newton writes that the Ultimate Reality has a value system of absolute love. Status, ego and ranking are not recognized, but rather the potential of each soul is developed. This development can be done by reincarnating on earth, but souls can also develop in the Ultimate Reality itself. However, being on earth seems to speed up the soul's development. Newton writes that part of our light energy always remains behind in the Ultimate Reality, even when we are on earth for a while.[59]

Life at the Ultimate Reality occurs in soul groups of three to twenty-five members who are made up of beings at about the same levels of advancement. No matter the level, souls are not seen as having less or more value compared to other souls. In the group there are soul mates and soul companions. Apparently souls become more physically beautiful when they are spiritually more advanced.[60]

Because it has no advantage for the soul's development to keep reincarnating into the same family, cultural environment and geographic setting, according to Michael Newton: "As a rule, members of the same soul group do not return in their next incarnations as members of the same genetic human family."[61]

Life Review, Life Book, Reason for Reincarnations
A "life review" may be part of a visit to the Ultimate Reality. According to Brian Weiss, this life review is done in a loving way, without judgment or criticism.[62] Michael Newton's subjects also speak of a council of Elders which assist in life review after death, and in choosing a next life. These Elders seem to be most sacred souls, according to Newton, accompanied by an all-knowing Presence (an Oversoul, they can be plural). Interesting to note is the fact that Newton's subjects do not refer to "God" when describing this Presence "as they feel as this word is too personalized on earth."[63]

Sylvia Browne refers to The Divine as a Force without a form or face.[64] She refers to these Elders in a similar manner as Newton. Brian Weiss calls these elders "the Masters."[65] These Masters/Elders discuss the life just completed, and may consult about the body and life chosen in the next reincarnation which serves to address karmic debts or work on specific lessons. It is therefore common for one to choose a less then perfect body or circumstances.

Karma is about learning, loving and forgiving, and not about punishment. It may take several lifetimes to master these. Michael Newton mentions that "rather then stages of punishment, we go through stages of self enlightenment."[66]

Sylvia Browne describes the different goals and challenges of our chart as Option Lines, of which there seem seven: health, spirituality, love, social life, finance, career, family. We usually choose one primary and one secondary option line for a life on earth.[67]

Each soul has what is called a Life Book, which includes all experiences of the soul. It can be reviewed for development of the soul, and is usually done so right after our return in the Ultimate Reality. This is very similar to the notion of the Akashic Record of Eastern religion. "Akasha" meaning the essence of all memory and energy that exists.[68] These Life Books seem to resemble vibrating sheets of energy that can form life hologram images of events, which can be entered and participated into. Souls are able to get into minds of others to feel what they felt at a certain moment. Scenes of our Life Book can be entered to experience it fully and learn from it. This to learn about empathy and to evaluate disruptive behavior of each other in past lives.[69] The place where Life Books are held is called the "Hall of Records", which is where we can review our lives and rewind certain parts for our personal development.[70]

In describing the sacred books of religion, Rosalind A. McKnight was explained that each one of us *is* a sacred book containing all knowledge and all reality in and of itself.[71] As written in the Koran, the illiterate Prophet Mohammad was also shown a "big book" by the angel identified as Gabriel who insisted three times for Mohammad to read it.[72] Coincidentally, Joseph Smith, the founder of the Mormon religion, was presented golden tablets with text. Shamans and (volunteer) subjects using psychedelics often speak of having been shown a book of knowledge by supernatural entities during AESC.

Patient quotes from Brian Weiss, Michael Newton and Sylvia Browne:
- Weiss: "Our task is to learn, to become God-like through knowledge. We know so little."[73] "They [the Masters] tell me there are many gods, for God is in each of us."[74] "There are many dimensions...That we must share our knowledge with other people."[75] "Yes, we choose when we will come into our physical state and

when we will leave. We know when we have accomplished what we were sent down here to accomplish. We know when the time is up, and you will accept your death...when you have had the time to rest and re-energize your soul, you are allowed to choose your re-entry back into the physical state."[76] "...we pick our family situations before birth in order to provide us with the greatest amount of growth possible."[77]

- Newton: "Souls come to earth to work on their own shortcomings."[78]

- Browne: "We each compose a detailed chart of our upcoming lifetime on The Other Side before we're born. Everything we experience here on earth, including our hardships and time of death, are ultimately of our own choosing, not His [The Divine]. We are at our most alive on The Other Side. Our brief trips to this dimension called earth are a decision we make, for the purpose of experiencing and overcoming negativity on our road toward perfecting our spirits for God. Our spirit remembers every birth, death, life on earth and life on The Other Side we've been through, and every new lifetime is deeply affected by those memories, whether we're consciously aware of them or not."[79] "..when we leave The Other Side for another incarnation, we arrive here to overcome specific challenges and accomplish specific goals, and we compose a detailed chart for our upcoming lives to help us realize those purposes."[80]

- Weiss: "Everybody's path is basically the same. We all must learn certain attitudes while we're in physical shape. Some of us are quicker to accept them then others. Charity, hope, faith...we must all know these things and know them well."[81] "We learn traits and qualities such as love, non-violence, compassion, charity, faith, hope, forgiveness, understanding and awareness. We must unlearn negative traits and qualities, including fear, anger, hatred, violence, greed, pride, lust, selfishness, and prejudice."[82] "Lifetimes are wisely and carefully scripted to enhance our learning and evolution."[83] "We choose our circumstances and establish a plan for our lives before we are even conceived."[84] "Destiny and free will co-exist and interact all the time. They are complementary, not contradictory."[85] "There are many levels of consciousness that we visit when our soul departs the physical body. One important level is the learning stage, where we review our lives. We re-experience every encounter, every relationship. We feel the emotions of the people whom we have helped or hurt, loved and hated, or affected positively or negatively. We feel their emotions very deeply, because this is a powerful learning device, a sort of instant intense feedback about our behavior while we were on earth, in physical bodies."[86]

Energy manipulation

Energy manipulation is part of the training souls receive in the Ultimate Reality. They do this out of an energy source provided for them. Souls can build and create by projected thoughts.[87]

Patient quotes from Michael Newton and Brian Weiss:
- Newton: "Souls learn to create and shape physical matter, such as rocks, soil, plants and lower life forms."[88] "After all, it was here [in the Ultimate Reality] where the conceptual design and eventual energy for physical organisms began."[89]
- Weiss: "My job is to change my level of consciousness and learn techniques of energy manipulation in order to transform matter."[90]

Earth is not the only world a soul can visit. According to Newton and Browne, other dimensions and worlds can be visited or used for soul growth. Newton has been told by his subjects that the Ultimate Reality is the true reality, and that earth is an illusion created to teach us. He also writes that: "Souls who travel inter-dimensionally explain that their movements appear to be in and out of curved spheres connected by zones that are opened and closed by converging vibrational attunement."[91]

RELIGION AND SCIENCE

Religious versus Mystical Experience

A mystical experience is defined in this book as having obtained the ultimate AESC called a pure consciousness state or mystical state. This experience may involve specific brain areas, which will be researched in this book. According to Timothy Leary a mystical experience goes together with an instant relief from emotional pressure.[1]

A religious experience will be defined in this book as involving rituals, traditions, established protocols and procedures, with as aim to worship. It involves participation of the entire body, as well as various non-specific brain areas. A religious experience most often does not involve an AESC, however, certain religious practices (meditation, prayer, drumming ritual or dance) may instill a mystical state or AESC.

Last century French sociologist Émile Durkheim wrote that although the apparent purpose of rituals is strengthening the ties between the faithful and their gods, what they really do is strengthen the ties between the individual and society. Durkheim is noted for stating that in all cultures, religion functions to sustain the moral order, and therefore religion is not a set of beliefs, but a set of practices, because these moral functions in turn may lack in spirituality.[2]

A mystical experience, or the state of pure consciousness, has been described to Rosalind A. McKnight by non-earthly beings as something that seems unreal in a real world, but that is actually the opposite, as it is the advancement of the soul into the truth of its reality and a signpost of growth.[3]

Post Modern Science versus Classical Newtonian Science

This book prefers a post modern approach towards scientific research. Issues related to the spiritual often cannot be scientifically quantified, as they often cannot be tested and challenged following the classical Newtonian model. The Newtonian model measures solid and material things that can be generally quantified with some or all of our five senses. It cannot measure consciousness or love, for example. Post modern scientists call for a new paradigm that includes these (unexplainable) phenomena in a more comprehensive theory of how the world works.[4] Numerous scientists and researchers join this approach.

Science professor John O.M. Bockris received his Ph.D. at the Imperial College of Science and Technology at the University of London, has been a full professor at the University of Pennsylvania, and at the Flinders University in Austrilia. Bockris has published 704 papers and 22 books about physics and other modern sciences to discuss (paranormal) phenomena such as: reincarnation, clairvoyance, OBE, ESP, healing at distance, etc. He also argues "science as religion", mathematics, relativity theory, quantum theory and the origin of life, and how these sciences fit these (paranormal) phenomena. John Bockris states, while referring to precognition and other psychical phenomena: "The refusal of most scientists to study these results arises principally because they believe that if the phenomenon cannot be explained by means of present theories of science, it does not exist."[5]

Andrew Newberg, Eugene d'Aquili and author Vince Rause: "Science concerns itself with that which can be weighed, counted, calculated, and measured – anything that can't be verified by objective observation simply can't be called scientific."[6] "Science, however, has not been able to empirically prove that mysticism is a product of distraught or dysfunctional minds. Significant research, in fact, seems to show that people who experience genuine mystical states enjoy much higher levels of psychological health than the public at large."[7] As example they write that those undergoing a spiritual experience describe these as ecstatic, joyful and often loving. This contrary to psychotics, who are often confused, distressed and frightened by their hallucinations.[8] "The organizing principle of science declares that everything that is real can be measured, and scientific methods are the only measurements that count."[9]

Andrew Newberg and Mark Robert Waldman write: "Science, too, is primarily based on causal beliefs, for if research does not make sense in some logical and reasonable way, other researchers will consider the conclusions false, or at best without merit, even if the results are actually true."[10]

Post modern scientists also argue that even though the scientific community may agree on an issue which is endorsed by governments and organizations, this does not guarantee that the consensus of the issue is correct.

Statistical data which shows that 72 percent of scientists (mainly biologists, mathematicians, physicists and astronomers) do not believe in God and only 7 percent does. The remaining 21 percent expressed religious doubt or is agnostic.[10]

The Brain

Brain and Mind
The brain is a physical organ that obtains and processes sensory, cognitive, and emotional information. The mind is the experience of thoughts, memories and emotions that arise from these brain processes. The two are intertwined, and similar as seen from different viewpoints.[1]

Rosalind A. McKnight writes that thoughts travel instantaneous, just by thinking of someone (dead or alive) they can pick up the thought. Since the mind is pure energy, what is thought can be brought instantly into reality. Emotions and stress can block thoughts and thus communication flow, as does fear. "Mind and emotions have a great deal to do with imbalance and disease."[2] And also: "The mind is an energy machine through which we create. We create our own circumstances... Everyone is a universe in and out of itself...There are no outer universes. The only universes that exist are universes that are perceived from within."[3]

Everything in the universe has an effect on everything else; everything and everyone has a purpose and meaning; all is one, and one is all; there is no "greater" and no "lesser"; the knowledge of everything is within us; the only limits put on our consciousness are those we put there ourselves (we are what we think).

The Brain
The brain, it is said, is for its size the most complex system known in the universe.[4] It is also the only organ capable of conscious perception.[5]

In general, the left hemisphere of our brain acts as the "talking half" (as source of active speech and words, language, writing, and of mathematical calculations) and as interpreter of our experienced world as seen from the outside, it is also considered analytical and rational. The right hemisphere – in general - is more the experiencer, and source of inside information (feelings, perceptions, spatial visualization and impressions). It is also considered integrative and holistic, and specializes in relations and the perception of distance.[6]

Overall, the right side interprets the wholeness of the world through feelings; the left side turns reality into ideas that can be communicated. Both sides work together to create a sense of reality that is different when formed by one side alone.[7]

Children's brains are not fully developed until late childhood or early teens and that the brain only develops properly through interaction, interplay and nurture by the caretaker. Research writers Carol Raush Albright and James B. Ashboork outline that the brain is very plastic, and that damaged or missing parts of one brain's hemisphere may be taken up by the other hemisphere (especially if this is the case in early childhood). They note that both hemispheres work close together, and that information passes back and forth between the two halves via the corpus callosum. Neither hemisphere is controlling nor dominant over the other. When the two hemispheres are disconnected, Albright and Ashbrook point out, both halves seem to have independent streams of consciousness.[8] Andrew Newberg and Mark Robert Waldman concur with this notion in their research.[9]

The autonomic nervous system is a part of the brain that is responsible for fundamental functions (heart rate, body temperature) and for emotional functions. The autonomic nervous system is divided into the sympathetic nervous system (arousal system, fight-or-flight response) and parasympathetic nervous system (relaxation, body balancing system and energy conservation system).[10]

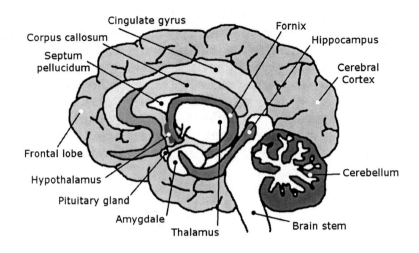

Section of the human brain

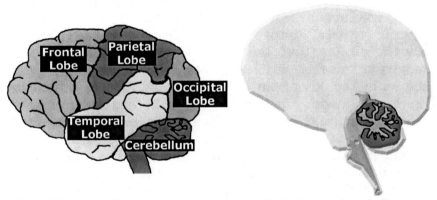

Lobes of the human brain   Brainstem and cerebellum

The Brain Stem and Cerebellum

The brain stem and cerebellum are also referred to as the reptilian brain, primal mind, or archipallium. The brain stem first occurred in reptiles and encompasses our basic behavior.[11]

The reptilian brain is involved in functions related to basic needs (protection, self-preservation or territory, reproduction, social structures, storage and foraging of food). These basic needs are in common with mammals, birds and reptiles.[12] The cerebellum is involved in the control and coordination of skeletal muscles.[13] The control center for dreaming is located in the reptilian brain and dreaming plays an important role to transfer stimuli from short-term input to long-term memory.[14]

Parts of the brainstem are the reticular activating system (RAS), raphe nuclei and locus coeruleus, which each play an important role in relaxation, meditation and prayer practices (See also appendix I – Brainstem). The raphe nuclei (Latin for 'the bit in a fold or seam'), are grouped into about nine pairs of nerve cell groups distributed along the entire length of the brainstem and release serotonin to the rest of the brain. The locus coeruleus (Latin for 'the blue spot' named after its color), is a nucleus in the brain stem responsible for physiological responses to stress and panic. This nucleus is one of the main sources of the stress hormone norepinephrine (= noradrenaline) in the brain, and is composed of mostly medium-sized neurons. RAS instigates changes in brainwave activity. It transmits facilitator signals to the thalamus, which in turn excites the cortex, which in return excites the thalamus, thus creating a reverberating circuit that makes make one wake up in the morning. RAS, thalamus, locus coeruleus and raphe nuclei together govern brainwave patterns.

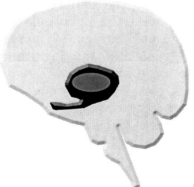

Limbic System

Limbic System
This system is also referred to as the old mammalian brain, emotional mind or brain, paleopallium, or fifth lobe. The

limbic system or limbic lobe controls smell, taste, and emotional responses. The limbic system adds emotions (love, joy, anger, fear) to the basic needs of guarding, mating and competing behavior, and motivates our attachments and desires. The outer arc is called the (limbic) gyrus.

The amygdale, hippocampus, thalamus and its small appendage hypothalamus are all part of the limbic system and are paired. Carol Raush Albright and James B. Ashbrook outline that emotions are linked with memory, and write that the limbic system has evolved certain functions not found in reptiles: "(1) Nursing and maternal care, (2) audio-vocal communication for maintaining maternal-offspring contract, and (3) play."[15]

In general in can be stated that the amygdala contains the seat of fear and anxiety, and is the control center for the display, storage and experience of emotions and moods. It is also responsible for dreams and emotional memories. The amygdala in turn activates the hypothalamus and hippocampus.

Broadly speaking, the thalamus is the processing center for sensory information (except smell), which it transmits to the cerebral cortex. It receives signals from RAS and then negotiates what state to be in, particularly when it comes to Alpha and Beta. Together with the hypothalamus it initiates sleep and levels of alertness (states of consciousness). It makes experiences feel real and lucid during meditation, prayer and spiritual regression hypnosis.

Overall, the hippocampus records experiences and arranges storage in long term memory, but does not directly generate emotion (unlike the amygdale and hypothalamus). However, it exerts great influence on an individual's state of mind as it balances the fear response of the amygdala. It is also a producer of slow wave, theta activity during REM.

Cerebral Cortex

The cerebral cortex is also referred to as the neocortex (new cortex), rational mind, or neopallium. The cerebral cortex lies around the top and sides of the brain. These areas are proportionately large in primates and human beings. Much of the cortex is designated to learning and synthesizing of information in a conscious way. The cerebral cortex performs most of the brain's higher cognitive functions. Contrary to the reptilian and mammalian brain, the cerebral cortex has the ability to communicate in speech. The cerebral cortex is divided into four lobes which are paired.[16]

Cerebral cortex

The frontal lobes consist of about one half of the brain. The frontal lobes have abundant connections with nearly every other part of the cortex and control motor activity and speech, but also are important for executive functions such as planning, pursuing long-term goals, judgment, self control, logic and clear thinking. The frontal lobes make it possible to express thoughts, ideas, emotions and complex speech. The prefrontal cortex (part of the frontal lobes), just behind the forehead, is the area where information from the body, from emotions, from memory, from thought and from holistic insight come together to create judgments and plans.[17]

The frontal areas are likely to be important in religious cognition.[18] The prefrontal cortex is the only area that receives input from all senses, including olfaction (smell).[19] Laurence O. McKinney writes that the prefrontal cortex is what made us humans fully conscious.[20]

The parietal lobes are located just behind the frontal lobes, are involved in processing sensory information and controls touch and position. The angular gyrus of the inferior parietal lobe and the frontal motor areas plays an important role in language, symbolic thinking, as well as artistry, drawing, creativity, tool use and manipulation. Apparently, hominoids and other non-human mammals, lack an angular gyrus (as it is unique to homo sapiens), and therefore have limited artistic talents, symbolic and tool-making abilities, Rhawn Joseph explains. Especially on the right hemisphere the angular gyrus plays a crucial role in carrying out artistic tasks.[21] Joseph is a neuroscientist and author of many books and extensive research articles on neurotheology. He obtained his doctorate from UHS/The Chicago Medical School, and completed his training at the VAMC/Yale University Medical School Seizure Unit, Department of Neurology, Neuropsychology Section.

The occipital lobes are located behind the parietal and temporal lobes at the back of the brain. They hold the brain's major visual-reception area.

The temporal lobes are located behind the frontal lobes and below the parietal lobes. They handle auditory processing (including understanding the spoken word), memory (due to the hippocampus) and the ability to recognize faces, geometric shapes and social emotional nuances (due to the amygdale).

Brainwave States
Brainwaves, or the EEG waves (Electro Encephalographic waves), are weak electrical signals that can be recorded from the brain, either directly or through the scalp. The brain generates these electric signals. Brainwave states indicate the dominant frequency at any given time. Even during these times other frequencies are still present. The brain hardly ever operates on just one frequency. Frequencies or cycles per second are measured in Hertz (Hz). One Hz is one oscillation per second (or one "wave" per second). Brain wave frequencies correlate with the states of our consciousness as per tables indicated on the next pages.

Brainwave State	Division	Frequency	Characteristics
Gamma Frequency 30-80 Hz			• Extreme hyper activity, stress and anxiety (rare state) • Gamma waves possibly play a role in binding sensory data through "neural firing", whereby impulses of high frequency "bind" (or brings together) vision, sight, sound, smell, touch to make sense of it all. • Short moments of precognition or high-level information processing.
Beta Frequency 13-30 Hz			• Normal waking state of mental activity and attention turned to our external environment. • Most people spend most waking hours in this state. • Higher beta is present during stress, anxiety, feelings of separation and flight or fight. • After an extended period in the Beta state the ration between potassium and sodium is out of balance resulting in mental fatigue.
	High	18-30 Hz	Focus
	Medium	15-17 Hz	Energy
	Low	13-14 Hz	Thinking
Alpha Frequency 8-12 Hz			• Relaxation state and attention turned inward, such as a calm and focused mental state or meditation, unwinding and letting go. Beginning of access to the unconscious mind. • Any frequency below 11 Hz apparently reduces stress. • Decrease in blood lactate levels.
	High	12	Self esteem
	Medium	10-11	Super learning
	Low	8-9	Memory, peak performance, attention focusing, meditation

Brainwave State	Division	Frequency	Characteristics
Theta 5-7 Hz			• 7.8 Hz is the resonant frequency of the Earth's magnetic field (also called Schumann Resonance which is between 6.8 and 8.3 Hz). • Deeper state of attention focusing and meditation. • Visualization and hypnagogic state before falling asleep. • Access to the subconscious mind, sensation of floating. • Resetting of the sodium/potassium levels in brain cells (related to rejuvenation of a fatigued brain). • Receptivity to suggestions on behavioral aspects. • Receptivity to new information. • Stress reduction. • Comprehension of advanced concepts and relationships. • Reminiscence of childhood experiences. • Increased intuitive, creative and psychic abilities. • Dreaming-sleep starts (REM rapid eye movement) with bursts to beta.
	High	7 Hz	Bliss, altered states
	Medium	6 Hz	Creativity, remote viewing, lucid dreaming
	Low	5 Hz	Serenity, tranquility, inspiration
Delta ½-4 Hz			• Delta is seen during (dreamless) sleep and at very experienced meditators. • Deepest states of attention focusing and meditation. • Access to the subconscious mind. • Deep insight and understanding. • Expanded awareness, visions and transpersonal experiences. • OBE (out of body experiences). • Deep delta triggers growth hormone release which is beneficial for healing and regeneration.
	High	4	Pain reduction
	Medium	2-3	Sleep, healing
	Low	½-1	Trance, deep rest, enlightenment

Table 4 – Brainwave States

PART II

TRAVEL MEANS & METHODS AND THEIR NEUROTHEOLOGICAL ASPECTS

TRAVEL ADVISORY

In order to have an enhanced possibility of success in achieving and exploring AESC and ODR, it is strongly suggested to use some or (preferably) all of the below listed advisories. It should be noted that there is *no guarantee* in achieving AESC, and no guarantee that you will indeed visit ODRs, even when all of the below advisories are used.

Exploring AESC and ODRs unprepared, is comparable to giving a sharp knife to a small child. When guided and well instructed, even a child can use the knife as a tool. It is therefore wise to take any voyage to another dimension seriously, and to be well prepared and informed. Actually, it is nothing different as if you would be taking a regular road-trip to a new destination.

The following advisories are important for any traveler:

1. <u>Get informed</u>
   Read up about your selected method of AESC and related ODRs through additional books and (web) articles by experts. Talk to seasoned travelers or experienced travel guides about their experiences. Inform yourself about the mental and physical mechanisms involved during the journey and their possible consequences.

2. <u>Free will and good motivation</u>
   Before you travel, it is of utmost importance that you are a willing and motivated participant of the voyage. If you have any doubts or uncertainties, don't jump into the deep-end, but obtain more information and knowledge first.

3. <u>Have a Travel Guide stand-by</u>
   It is highly recommendable to have a skilled travel guide

present as an observer who remains in a normal wakened state during the entire duration of your voyage. The role of the guide will be providing assistance or encouragement if and when required. The travel guide could also make notes during the voyage if you are able to voice you experiences en-route. After the journey you could discuss these observations with the travel guide.

4. Food, drink and toilet
   Go to the toilet prior to commencing your voyage to avoid an unpleasant pit-stop that interrupts your travel experience. At the same time, do not start your journey on an empty stomach, but eat a small meal before hand. Avoid alcohol and cigarettes for a day prior to your journey.

5. Prepare your inner self
   To enhance the likelihood of a pleasurable voyage, several preparatory techniques are very useful, such as affirmations, relaxation techniques, controlled breathing, visualizations, etc. Experience in meditation is not required, but helps in calming the mind prior to departure.

6. Prepare your environment
   To enhance a smooth departure, your direct environment should be as calm as possible. Try to refrain from bright light, noise and interruptions. The environment should be comfortable of climate. Your physical position should be comfortable and free from muscular stress. Loose clothing prevents physical discomfort during the voyage. Make sure the clothing keep your feet and body warm.

7. Eliminate fear
   Fear is the foremost obstacle to a positive outcome of your travels. Therefore all of the previously mentioned advisories are to be taken seriously. There is nothing to be afraid of, yet it is easier said then done. When you are well prepared, you can easily put fear on the side lines and have a wonderful travel experience.

8. <u>Recap</u>

   Afterward, discuss the voyage (and possible notes) with your travel guide, and record these as reference to future travels and to provide information to fellow travelers.

PSYCHEDELICS

Travel Method

Psychedelics may also be referred to in popular literature as hallucinogenics, or in scientific literature as entheogens ("God" inducing drugs). Psychedelics are not physiologically addictive, contrary to amphetamines (ecstasy), cocaine and opioids (opium, heroine, morphine, codeine, and methadone). The better known psychedelics are: ayahuasca (DMT), psilocybin (magic mushrooms), LSD, iboga, and mescaline (peyote). Psychedelics are not physically addictive either, unlike opioids. DMT has no tolerance development, and can be frequently repeated again to achieve at each occasion a similarly intense experience and in-depth result.

Psychedelics affect all senses, and have the effect that reality becomes uncensored. For example, it is possible that sights can be smelled and sounds can be seen. There seem to be several ODRs that can be experienced when using psychedelics. When using psychedelics, 40-90% of subjects undergo an intense mystical or revelatory experience; 40-75% have an intense and life-changing experiences; 40-90% of these experiences will be revelatory.[1]

There is an argument that drugs cannot create new experiences that we have never had before, and that drugs can only enhance or suppress those capacities we already possess.[2] This statement is disputed by other researchers who distinguish ODR from (earthly) human realities, because the brain often creates images that do not exist in the world.[3] Furthermore, sound apparently can create visual images in our brain that do not actually exists.[4]

The use of plants to induce AESC probably started by the earliest known Homo Sapiens called Cro-Magnon in the Upper

Paleolithic period of the Pleistocene era (starting 40,000 to 30,000 years ago). Altered states and Upper Paleolithic (religious) art are related and appeared first as cave-art in France (Chauvet, Lascaux, Pech Merle) and Spain (Altamira). Plant-induced visions of shamans are depicted in this cave art. This neuropsychological theory was first formulated by cave-art specialist David Lewis-Williams. Plant and fungi species with psychedelic properties are found in abundance all over the world. Access to supernatural realms through these visions provided the first basis of life after death, and henceforth spirituality.[5]

Terence McKenna explains that pre-Buddhist shamans and yogis were avid hash smokers and/or users of datura (local Indian-Tibetan herb).[6] He also states that: "..most shamanism that is vital *is* hallucinogenic-plant shamanism. A shaman's foremost tool is obtaining ecstasy."[7] "Shamanism worldwide insists that the universe is multileveled, populated by beings that can do you great good, do you great harm. And beings who don't give a hoot about you, one way or the other."[8]

AESC obtained by San Bushmen in South Africa are the works of sacred plants, and that these AESC-experiences are expressed through dance, singing and artwork (going back to 26,000 years BC). Rock art of these Bushmen are their record of AESC. Current day Bushmen rely on hyperventilation, deep concentration and rhythmic dancing instead of psychedelics to obtain AESC.[9]

A shaman can be defined as someone who enters an AESC (also known as magical soul flight) to communicate with the spirits on behalf of the community and also to heal members of the community. This AESC or soul journey is not a possession. Cross-cultural studies have revealed many similarities among healing practices of shamans, including AESC.[10]

The shrine of Eleusis (near Athens, Greece) celebrated the myth of Dementer and Persephone, whereby Dementer goes to the underworld to claim back the soul of her daughter. This myth can be compared with the death and rebirth of a shamanic mission during AESC. The shrine became known for the visions that visitors would have. It became a pilgrimage destination until the Christians closed the shrine in the fourth century AD. It appears that pilgrims visiting the shrine were obliged to drink a potion called kykeon, containing barley and mint, which often bears the fungal parasite ergot which has psychedelic properties (Albert Hoffman synthesized LSD from the same fungus). Aristotle and Plato are known to have visited this shrine.[11]

The psychoactive fungus Claviceps Purpurea may have been the ergot. Its purple color was represented in the purple robes of the priests. This fungus grows throughout Europe.[12]

According to Professor of Psychology Benny Shanon of the Hebrew University in Jerusalem, Ezekiel's visions of "opening the heavens and seeing God" are comparable to ayahuasca induced visions of opening heavens, and celestial and heavenly scenes. Ezekiel's vision of therianthropic creatures (part man, part animal) is consistent with a psychedelic AESC experience. Psychedelic plants do grow in the Middle Eastern region.[13]

Dr. Rick Strassman has performed one of the last Drug Enforcement Administration (DEA)-approved clinical research on DMT. He writes that the psychedelic substance DMT is produced by the pineal gland in our own bodies, and states that as an endogenous psychedelic it may be involved in naturally occurring AESC states (such as spontaneous trance, UFO abductions, OBE, NDE, etc.). Because of the similarities between UFO abduction stories and AESC induced by DMT, it is possible that UFO abduction experiences occur to people who spontaneously overproduce DMT at times.[14]

According to a 1975 study by Reickel-Dolmatoff, there are several stages that can be visited during plant or mushroom induced AESC (described as the different ODRs in this book). These similar stages are depicted by cave art expert David Lewis-Williams. Some or all of these ODRs occur in random order during AESC induced by psychedelics according to volunteers in a laboratory setting. Transition from one ODR to another apparently overlaps smoothly (for example: geometric and iconic patterns fade into hybrid entities, who in turn transform into humanoids) and are not necessarily sequentially. The environment experienced during AESC can be either deep underground, under water or above ground. Sensations and realities undergone during plant or fungi induced AESC are very similar when comparing historical accounts to current day experiences. They are all perceived as very real.[15]

Rick Strassman states that many volunteers indicated lucid awareness of experiencing their environment during AESC, as they commented that they "looked around and saw.."[16]

The transition from earth to ODR often is accompanied with humming sounds, bright light, body vibrations and high speed travel. Encounters with non-earthly intelligent beings are known. Knowledge may also be transferred by insight in "sacred books".

Besides the abundant accounts of similarities in the various ODRs, there are also differences. Besides loss of (normal) time/space and telepathic communication, the similarities between the ODRs visited typically are listed below:

- Geometric ODR : reachable through most psychedelics.

- Hybrid ODR: reachable through DMT and psilocybin. With LSD, mescaline, peyote and iboga it seems possible but less evident to reach to this reality. Snakes appear universal during an Ayahuasca-DMT-induced visit.

- Humanoid ODR: reachable through DMT and psilocybin. With LSD, iboga, mescaline and peyote it seems unlikely to reach this reality.

- Ultimate Reality: Psychedelic explorer Terence McKenna explains that he much prefers psilocybin and DMT over

LSD and mescaline, as the effect is so much more powerful and real. He claims that DMT is by far the strongest psychedelic, in which other entities can be seen. Even though it does not last long (five minutes at its peak), the body and mind recuperate rather fast (approx. 20 minutes) and tolerate it well, as there is no physical or physiological dependence. However, his personal preference is the psilocybin mushroom, as the experience is sustained for a couple of hours instead of a couple of minutes with DMT. He also outlines that psilocybin and ayahuasca (DMT containing brew) both produce a telepathic experience and a shared state of mind, whereby every participant is seeing the same thing.[17]

McKenna writes: "Ayahuasca seemed a hallucinogen with less of the internally self-organized quality that characterizes mushroom psilocybin, which seems to show that the psilocybin experience is not so much self-exploration as an encounter with an organized Other."[18] He continues: "Unlike the psilocybin rapture, which presents itself as an alien intelligence, the ayahuasca seemed to have a kind of psychiatric presence that urged the recognition that all images and powers of the Other spring from our confrontation with ourselves. Like the psilocybin mushroom, it displayed a network of information that seemed to make accessible the experiences and images if many worlds, but ayahuasca insisted that in some sense still unrevealed these were ultimately human worlds."[19]

Another known (historical) psychedelic is the blue water lily (Nymphaea Caerulea) which was used in Mayan and ancient Egyptian rituals. It was often soaked for a few days in (palm) wine prior to consumption

Mandrake (Mandgranora Officinarum) is another plant known in Egypt and Europe with hallucinogenic properties.

Further, there is the legendary Soma or Haoma, as described in the ancient Indian Vedic scriptures. It is not certain which plant or fungus is referred to by Soma, but it could possibly be the fungus Amanita Muscaria. This fungus retains its properties in the urine of the user and can be recycled up to five times. Morning Glory seeds were used during Mayan rituals, and seem to have LSD like properties. Other, lesser known, psychedelic plants are Datura, Jimsonweed (Datura stramonium), Henbane, Belladonna, Salvia (Salvia Divinorum).

Anthropologist and writer Jeremy Narby studied history at the University of Canterbury, and received a doctorate in anthropology from Stanford University. He has done a lot of research regarding shamanic AESC. He writes that certain psychedelic brews of the Amazon region are very longwinded and complicated and include a variety of different plant species and cooking methods. He finds it hard to imagine that these brews were found by chance.[20] He further writes: "So here are people without electron microscopes who choose, among some 80,000 Amazonian plants species, the leaves of a bush containing a hallucinogenic brain hormone, which they combine with a vine containing substances that inactivate an enzyme of the digestive tract which would otherwise block the hallucinogenic effect. And they do this to modify their consciousness. It is as if they knew about the molecular properties of plants *and* the art of combining them, and when one asks them how they know these things, they say their knowledge comes directly from hallucinogenic plants."[21]

The ayahuasca brew consists of several ingredients. One of these is Psychotria viridis (which has the DMT). DMT gets destroyed by a stomach enzyme. The Amazon shamans figured out to combine this plant with Banisteriopsis caapi to avoid DMT destruction by this stomach enzyme. Amazonian shamans claim they have been taught everything by a variety of plant spirits.[22] Coincidentally, many herbal recipes seem not to work in a healing process if they were not instructed by a plant spirit encountered by a shaman during AESC. At the same time it is known that the context in which psychedelics are taken have a profound effect on the outcome of the trip.

John O.M. Bockris: "Correspondingly, Marie and Costelle in 1993 have pointed out that some scenes of glorious landscapes etc. reported by LSD imbibers are similar to some of the content found in reports from NDE's."[23] "What is not generally known is that scientific, controlled work on the effects of carefully measured doses of LSD (or alternatively, electrical stimulation of parts of the brain), give rise to reports which suggest that there are higher states of awareness available to people, and attainable by the use of chemical or electrochemical stimulation, or a long-lasting ascetic practice."[24]

Timothy Leary: "There is haunting phenomenological evidence that spiritual insights accompanying the psychedelic experience might be *subjective accounts* of the objective findings of astronomy, physics, biochemistry and neurology."[25] Leary states that almost any LSD tripper reports that genetic stages (unfolding of DNA) are visualized. Biologist Sir Francis Crick, who received the Nobel Prize with James Watson after revealing the structure and double helix of deoxyribonucleic acid (DNA) admitted prior to his death that he was on an LSD trip when the double helix shape and DNA structure were revealed to him. Contrary to popular belief, psychedelics create overall more positive then negative experiences. Apparently the attitude of the user is very important. Fear and anxiety contribute to a negative experience. "Letting go" and trust creates a positive experience. Leary outlines that a psychedelic experience should not be taken lightly and should be well prepared. Scheduling, meditation, the setting and the time of day are all very important preparatory factors to take into consideration. He also advises for one person to remain with the experiencer as an observer, helper and guide during the trip. He notes that negative (LSD) reactions during a psychedelic experience are based on the persons individual fears. As advice he notes that stomach messages during the experience should be noted as a sign that consciousness is moving around in the body.[26]

Psychedelics Overview	
Common name	**Chemically active compound** **Tryptamine family & information**
DMT "Dimitri" Access to Geometric, Hybrid, Humanoid ODR and possibly the Ultimate Reality	N,N-dimethyl-<u>tryptamine</u> Naturally released by our pineal gland. When natural levels are exceeded (including due to outside intake) unusual experiences and AESC take place. Natural substance from the South American Psychotria viridis plant. Gives a 30-60 minute total effect, with a 5-minute peak. Simplest of the tryptamine psychedelics. A cocktail of South American plants gives the Ayahuasca brew, consisting of: Psychotria viridis (which has the DMT) combined with Banisteriopsis caapi (which contains a beta-carboline which prevents destruction of DMT in our stomachs by our enzyme monoamine oxidase). Sometimes the plant datura is added to the brew. Unlike LSD, psilocybin and mescaline, DMT has no tolerance development.
Psilocybin "Magic mushrooms" Access to Geometric, Hybrid, Humanoid ODR	4-phosphoraloxy-N,N-dimethyl-<u>tryptamine</u> Natural substance from the Psilocybin mushroom. Gives 30 min to 4-8 hour trip. Examples North American fungi: Panaeolus sphinctrinus, Panaeolus campanulatus, Panaeolus papilonaceus. Northern European fungi (±30 species). Psilocybe semilanceata (a mushroom species). Various Panaeolus species found on herbivore dung.

Common name	Chemically active compound Tryptamine family & information
Iboga "Eboka" Access to Geometric ODR	Ibogaine Hydrochloride or 12-Methoxyibogamine (contains a <u>tryptamine</u> core) Natural substance from the Tabernanthe iboga, a root bark from Africa. Gives 12-24 hour effect. Ironically, in clinical trials it has been reported that one dose - or at the most intermittent doses over two years – can instantly remove the destructive addiction of several hard drugs, such as cocaine and heroin, and even alcohol and nicotine.
LSD "Acid" "Yellow sunshine" Access to Geometric ODR	D-Lysergic Acid Diethylamide (contains a <u>tryptamine</u> core) Laboratory created substance. Gives 6-12 hours effect. First synthesized from the fungus ergot, a rye fungus, by Albert Hoffmann in 1938. Known to have a strong beneficial effect on creativity.
Mescaline "Peyote" Access to Geometric ODR	3,4,5-trimethoxy-beta-<u>phenethylamine</u> Natural substance from the North American Peyote cactus. Gives trip up to 12 hours.

Common name	Chemically active compound Tryptamine family & information
Serotonin (5-HT)	5-hydroxy-<u>tryptamine</u> <u>This is not a psychedelic,</u> but the most important neurotransmitter of our brain, and found in all plant and animal life. Note close relationship to the tryptamines DMT and Psilocybin. It also contains a similar to s tryptamines core as LSD and iboga. These psychedelics can block or mimic the effects of serotonin. The brain seems to fancy DMT, which it also produces. The body allows DMT, Psilocybin, LSD and iboga to replace serotonin in its receptor sites, which are widespread throughout the body. When blocking serotonin in its function, the amygdala increases its activity. In the brain these receptor sites are involved in mood, perception and thought.
Melatonin	5-methoxy-N-acetyl-<u>tryptamine</u> <u>This is not a psychedelic</u> but a neurotransmitter. It is found in all living creatures. Within the pineal gland, serotonin is acetylated and then methylated to yield melatonin. Induced melatonin produces a slight sedation and relaxation response only.

Table 5 – Psychedelics Overview

What Happens in the Brain

Serotonin-transmission blockers (such as LSD) result in increased activity in the sensory pathways to the neocortex. He continues that administration of LSD is followed by theta waves. Bursts of paroxysmal spike discharges occur in the hippocampus and amygdale. When in humans and chimps the (right) temporal lobes, amygdale and hippocampus are removed, LSD no longer produces hallucinations.[27] Psilocybin and DMT work directly on the language centers.[28]

DMT is found in human blood, brain tissue and cerebrospinal fluid, and AESCs are unleashed when naturally occurring DMT levels are raised above a certain threshold in laboratory volunteers.[29]

DMT is produced naturally in our pineal gland by a conversion process of serotonin. The first release of DMT seems to occur in a fetus at approximately forty-nine days after conception.[30]

Rick Strassman writes that when DMT was administered intravenously during his research, heart rate and blood pressure augment and pituitary gland hormones increase rapidly (for example beta-endorphin, which is a morphine-like chemical that provides an ecstatic feeling). Strassman also concluded that the brain hormones vasopressin and prolactin increase (these are seemingly important in feelings of bonding, attachment and comfort with others). He found that also growth hormone and corticotrophin increase. Corticotrophin stimulates the adrenal glands, which then release the stress steroid cortisal. However, Strassman writes, melatonin (produced in the pineal gland) did not increase. It is possible, he continues, that exogenous DMT stimulates the pineal to make more endogenous DMT. Since melatonin is also made by the pineal gland out of serotonin, it seems that DMT production receives priority in this case. Strassman also states that subjects who received a big dose of DMT were very suggestible, open and vulnerable. Another side effect, he writes, is the onset of nausea during AESC (this was described also by Leary). He explains this to be a way for the body to distract us from anxiety and sadness (it is easier to feel sick then sad), or that nausea may relate to something deep personal we are not ready to face. Strassman also noticed that several volunteers who received a high-dose DMT showed REM (rapid eye movement, as seen during dreamtime in sleep). He suggests that DMT may induce a wakeful dream state, only to be contradicted by his subjects who clearly indicate that their experiences was far from being a dream. He then questions if imagination could generate a more-then-real-life-experience.[31]

Meditation and Prayer

Travel Method
Andrew Newberg and the late Eugene d'Aguili have been the predominant researchers on the neurological effects of meditation and prayer since the late 1980ies. During their years of research (which is continuing by Newberg after Aguili's death in 1998) they have searched to understand brain functions during AESC and states of pure consciousness obtained by meditation and prayer.

They performed AESC research of Tibetan Buddhist monks during meditation and Franciscan nuns during prayer. The researchers describe two different methods of meditation or AESC: passive ("eastern") and active ("western"). During the passive approach the objective is to clear the mind. This technique utilized by the Tibetan monks is autonomous whereby the individual uses their own will to initiate and maintain a practice (this in contrast to guided meditations, whereby practitioners are verbally assisted). The monks describe their state of pure consciousness as oneness with the universe and a loss of self into something grander. Psychiatrist and Regression Therapist Brian Weiss identifies passive meditation as "keeping the mind completely blank, in a state of mindfulness or awareness, free to accept whatever feelings, ideas, images, or visions enter it and letting associations flow to all aspects of the object or thought – to understand its form, shape, color, essence".[1]

During the active approach one focuses on an object. The neurological functions of these meditations are similar to praying to, for example, Jesus or Maria, with as end-goal pure consciousness in the form of oneness with The Divine (also called Unio Mystica).[2] Brian Weiss explains active meditation as "contemplation": meaning concentrating on a specific subject – the idea of loving kindness, for example, or the beauty of a butterfly. He further emphasizes that it is easier for the Western mind to practice contemplation, as we are used to focusing, thinking and analyzing. Weiss writes that passive meditation is more of an Eastern concept which requires months or years of practice.[3]

Rosalind A. McKnight describes prayer as "talking to God, or giving", while meditation was described as "listening to God, or receiving." Prayer and visualization have healing power.[4]

Andrew Newberg and Eugene d'Aguili write that the perception of space and time can be significantly distorted during AESC. They describe three characteristics of AESC due to meditation or prayer. First, there is a sense of transcendence or otherworldliness. Second, there is the incorporation of the observing self. Third is the combination of the first two, and which transcends above our objective reality (as an example Newberg and d'Aguili mention one category of AESC, the NDE - near death experiences).[5]

They also write about NDE: "What is important here, however, is that almost all individuals who have had a complete core experience, especially involving the realm of light and the life review, are absolutely certain of the objective reality of their experience. This is not only among educated persons, but even among the most educated philosophers and scientists. This is apparently true among neuroscientists as well. Furthermore, people who have had the core NDE no longer appear to fear death. And the lives of near death experiencers are nearly always dramatically changed in the direction of increased altruism and a generally more benevolent attitude towards family, friends, and indeed the world."[6]

Newberg and d'Aguili conclude that those persons having undergone a state of pure consciousness (during meditation, prayer, or otherwise) seem absolutely certain that they have been in direct contact with The Divine. They seem to be certain of the realness of the ODR presented in this mystical state, which may include convincing presences in the form of non-earthly intelligent beings. Therefore, they continue, the reality of these states should be considered real; otherwise the term "reality" seems to have no meaning whatsoever.[7]

What Happens in the Brain

Research of Penfield and Perot in 1963 suggested that religious and spiritual activities were connected with the limbic stem of the brain.[8]

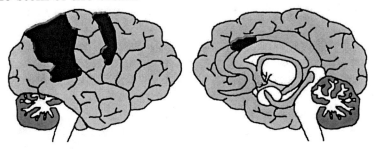

Brain areas most active during meditation (black)

When well seasoned monks and nuns achieve pure consciousness during their AESC séance, SPECT scans are taken to monitor activity centers in different brain areas. SPECT scans stand for single positron emission computerized tomography, which are scans that result in three-dimensional images, indicating activity centers of the brain during the achievement of the mystical states of monks and nuns.[9]

According to Newberg and d'Aguili: "..the SPECT scans hinted at the ability to interpret spiritual experiences as real, because of the mind's capacity to enter AESC and to adjust its assessment of reality neurologically."[10]

Prior to the scan and the séance, the participants are inserted with a radioactive tracer. The scans pointed to an increased activity in the dorsal lateral prefrontal cortex (part of the frontal lobes corresponding to intense and maintained concentration and attention), cingulated gyrus and thalami; and a decrease (blocking) in activity in mainly the left hemispheric posterior superior parietal lobe (part of the frontal lobes corresponding to the fading of self into non-self). The posterior superior parietal lobe is located at the top rear section of the brain is responsible to orient the individual in physical space. Also, there is a decrease in activity in parts of the inferior parietal lobe, and possible adjacent areas of the brain (in particular when all these are on the non-dominant side of the brain). fMRI and PET scans by Newberg and d'Aguili confirm their SPECT findings (increase of activity in the prefrontal cortex and decrease in activity in the parietal regions). Practitioners of verbally guided meditations did <u>not</u> show any increased frontal lobe activity.

During meditation or prayer, when focusing on a specific belief or object, the amygdale activates → the thalamus makes it feel real → the frontal lobes consciously interprets it → the hippocampus records the belief or notion → storage in long term memory. This process in itself does not prove that something is real or not.[11]

When practicing Franciscan nuns and Buddhist practitioners were resting, their left thalamus was more active then the other. This asymmetric activity is highly unusual, and only found in those with neurological damage, which these nuns and monks did not have. People practicing informal meditation practices do not have this asymmetry. This asymmetrical activity between the two thalami suggests, according to Andrew Newberg and Mark Robert Waldman: "..either that the people we have been scanning are born with a unique capacity to have spiritual revelations, or that they have altered their neural functioning in permanent ways as a result of years of intensive practice."[12]

Newberg and d'Aguili describe two different methods of meditation: active and passive.[13] The asymmetric blood flow between the frontal lobes and posterior superior parietal lobe (front and middle of the brain) could explain the pure consciousness state.[14]

Newberg and d'Aguili identify four states related to AESC and the state of pure consciousness:

1. Hyperquiescence (related to the parasympathetic nervous system) – state of extraordinary relaxation (sleep or meditation).

2. Hyperarousal (related to the sympathetic nervous system) – state of arousal, excitation and fierce concentration (marathon runners, rapid ritual dancing).

3. Hyperquiescence with Arousal Breakthrough – spillover from parasympathetic to sympathetic nervous system during, for example, great bliss when overflow creates a rush of energy (Buddhists call this the Appana Samahdi state, when the meditator becomes one with the object he was concentrating on).

4. Hyperarousal with Quiescent Breakthrough – spillover from the sympathetic to the parasympathetic nervous system during, for example, a trancelike state which is experienced as an ecstatic rush of orgasmic like energy (after for example rapid ritualistic dancing – see also Chapter 6 – Repetitive and Rhythmic Stimulation). [15]

There is a difference between neural functions during mentally induced trance (see Tables 10-13) and physically induced trance (such as rhythmic dancing combined with drumming and singing, see also Chapter 6, Tables 16 and 17).[16]

Scott Atran received his PhD in anthropology from Columbia University. While a student he became assistant to anthropologist Margaret Mead at the American Museum of Natural History. Because religious beliefs and experiences cannot be proven, validation occurs through interpreting (strong) emotions associated with religion. Atran quotes Schmidt and Trainor to give an example: "Electro cortical measures of frontal brain activity suggest that people exhibit greater relative left frontal activity to joyful and happy music and greater relative right frontal activity to fearful and sad music, with activity greater for fearful than sad reactions, and for joyful than happy reactions."[17]

It appears, he writes, that emotional stress associated with death seems a stronger motivator for religiosity then for example emotions associated with praying. Emotionally charged experiences apparently have a stronger impact on belief in the supernatural."[18]

Mystical states may be stimulated voluntarily or involuntarily. They depend on the differential stimulation of limbic system, (hypothalamus, hippocampus, and amygdale, as well as the right frontal and right temporal lobe). It seems that these parts of the brain contribute to religious and emotional experience.[19]

The hypothalamus is mainly concerned with raw emotions, homeostasis and hormonal aspects related to violent behavior and sexual activity. The amygdale also plays a role in violent behavior and sexual activity, together with the temporal lobe and hippocampus, and that these enable religious, spiritual and mystical experiences. Both the hypothalamus and amygdale are pleasure centers that contain opiate producing neurons and opiate (encephalin) receptive neurons, producing lows and highs. The amygdale has large concentrations of these encephalin producing neurons. High concentrations of opiates can eventually induce calm states and euphoria. Encephalin, also spelled as encephalin, is a natural opiate hormone and one of several naturally occurring morphine-like substances (called endorphins).[20]

Brain scanning method	Definition	What it determines or measures
MRI	Magnetic Resonance Imaging	Structural changes in the brain
fMRI	Functional Magnetic Resonance Imaging	Structural changes in the brain
CT	X-ray computed tomography	Structural changes in the brain
SPECT	Single Photon Emission Computed Tomography (subject is inserted with a radioactive tracer)	Changes in blood flow, metabolism and neurochemical activity
PET	Positron Emission Tomography (subject is inserted with a radioactive tracer)	Changes in blood flow, metabolism and neurochemical activity

Table 6 – Brain scanning methods

Brain activity during mystical states obtained during meditation and prayer		
Brain Area	Activity	Result
Amygdala	Increased	strengthening pleasant emotions
Thalamus	Increased	having a lucid experience making the experience feel real
Dorsal lateral prefrontal cortex, cingulated gyrus and thalami	Increased	general interpretation of the feeling of the experience intense and maintained concentration and attention
Posterior superior parietal (mainly left hemisphere) Parts of inferior parietal lobe (mainly left side)	Decreased	fading of self into non-self decreased sense of self and other decreased sense of space and time overall sense of unity among discrete objects
Hippocampus	Increased	recording of the experience storage of the experience into long-term memory

Table 7 – Brain activity during mystical states

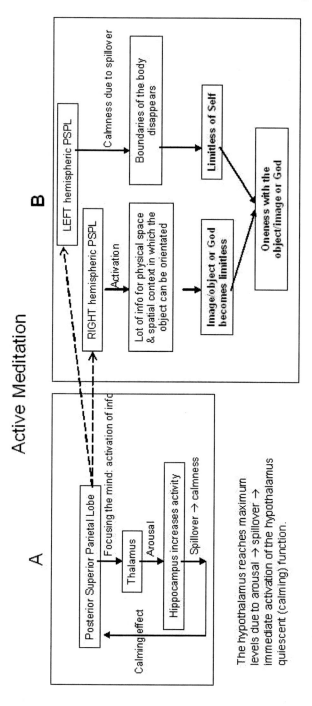

Table 8 – Active "Western" meditation

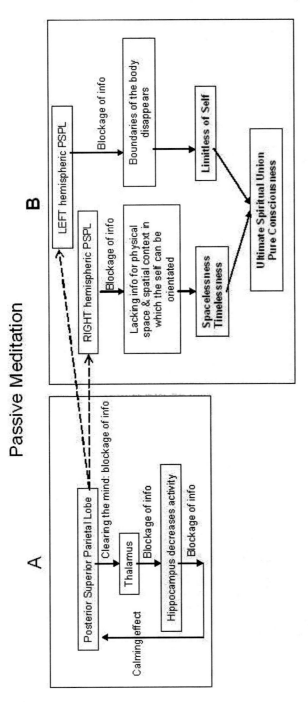

Table 9 – Passive "Eastern" meditation

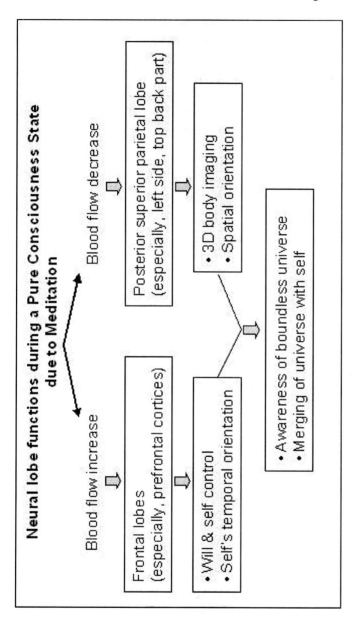

Table 10 – Neural lobe functions during a Pure Consciousness State due to Meditation

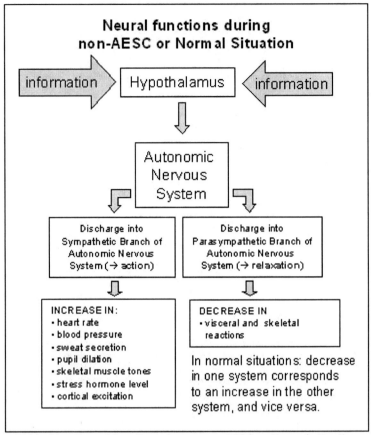

Table 11 – Neural functions during non-AESC or Normal situation

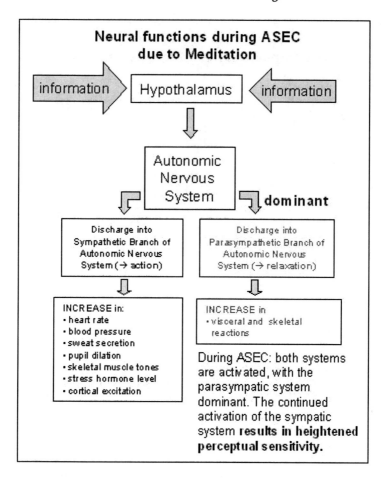

Table 12 – Neural functions during AESC due to Meditation

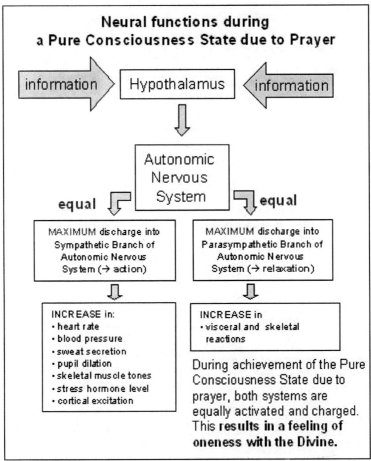

Table 13 – Neural functions during a Pure Consciousness
State due to Prayer

Neurochemical changes observed during meditation and related spiritual practices		
Neuro-chemical	**Change**	**Production and utilization**
AVP arginine vasopressin	Increased significantly	Produced in the supraoptic nucleus of the hypothalamus has various functions: tightens blood vessels, decreases self-perceived fatigue and arousal, improves consolidation of new memories and learning, provides a general positive effect.
GABA gamma aminobutyric acid	Increased	Neurotransmitter: principal inhibitor in the brain, may inhibit specific brain functions during meditation.
Melatonin	Increased significantly	Neurohormone produced by the pineal gland, which converts serotonin into melatonin when innervated by the lateral hypothalamus. Melatonin depresses the central nervous system and reduces pain sensitivity.
Serotonin	Increased	Neuromodulator influences flow of visual associations generated by the temporal lobe. Low levels of serotonin are associated with depression, higher levels have a positive effect and result in increased relaxation.
Cortisol	Decreased	Hormone associated with stress response, produced when the paraventricula nucleus of the hypothalamus secretes CRH (corticotrophin releasing hormone) in response to release of NE (norepinephrine). In turn CRH stimulates the anterior pituitary to release ACTH (adrenocorticotropic hormone), which in turn stimulates the adrenal cortex to produce Cortisol.

Neurochemical changes observed during meditation and related spiritual practices, continued		
Neuro-chemical	**Change**	**Production and utilization**
NE norepinephrine /noradrenaline and epinephrine (adrenaline)	Decreased	Neuromodulator and stress hormone produced by the locus cereleus of the pons. Along with epinephrine usually affects the flight-or-fight response, activating the sympathetic nervous system to directly increase heart rate, release energy from fat, and increase muscle readiness. Studies concluded that the relaxation response techniques (such as meditation and prayer) reduces the central nervous system's response to norepinephrine.
BE beta-endorphin	Rhythm changed, levels unaltered	Endogenous opioid produced mainly by the arcuate nucleus of the medial hypothalamus and distributed into the subcortical areas. BE depresses respiration, reduces fear and pain. It produces sensations of joy and euphoria.

Table 14 – Neurochemical changes during meditation and related spiritual practices

REGRESSION HYPNOSIS

Travel Method

Even though regression hypnosis is mainly used for healing purposes, its process allows for obtaining AESC and for access to the Ultimate Reality. Psychiatrists and hypnotists have encountered many descriptions of the Ultimate Reality through their patients, and have attained insight to life "on the other side". Travels to the Humanoid ODR have also been documented.

Psychologist Dr. Arthur Janov writes that hypnosis disintegrates consciousness, thereby achieving dissociation. Janov is the originator of primal therapy which has as thesis that both physical and psychic ailments can be linked to early trauma. According to Janov, hypnosis is viewed as a direct route to the subconscious, where traumas can be relived and resolved without any conscious participation. Janov further explains that hypnosis' "past-life regression" (which had been practiced since the 1860s, if not earlier, in Europe) holds as thesis that events and problems in past lives can generate issues and symptoms in this life. Thus, through hypnosis, one can gain access to past identities.[1] He states: "Although professional hypnosis organizations have condemned past-life regression, it has made its way into Ericksonian hypnotherapy, the school based on the work of Milton Erickson (1902-1980), the pre-eminent hypnotist in recent decades. Some hypnotists have even been able to induce "age progression," in which patients conjure up themselves in the future for ostensible therapeutic benefit."[2] "Erickson believed that hypnosis was a special state of highly-focused attention. During this state, the conscious mind could be shifted, transformed, or bypassed with relative ease, making unconscious memories more accessible than during a normal waking states."[3]

Hypnosis used for healing seems most effective when the mind is in alpha state.

Psychiatrist Brian Weiss writes that the state between wakefulness and sleeping is known as the hypnagogic state.[4] He identifies hypnosis as a state of focused concentration.[5] Weiss also writes about hypnosis: "When you are hypnotized, you are not asleep. Your conscious mind is always aware of what you are experiencing while you are hypnotized. Despite the deep subconscious contact, your mind can comment, criticize and censor. You are always in control what you say. Hypnosis is *not* a truth serum...No person I have ever hypnotized has become "stuck" in the hypnotic state. You can emerge from a state of hypnosis whenever you want...In hypnosis, your mind is always aware and observing...If the year 1900 flashes, and you find yourself building a pyramid in ancient Egypt, you *know* that the year is B.C., even if you don't see those actual letters."[6] Weiss continues: "All hypnosis is really self-hypnosis in that you, the patient, control the process. The therapist is merely a guide. Most of us enter hypnosis states every day – when we are absorbed in a good book or movie, when we have driven our car to the last few blocks home without realizing how we got there, whenever we have been on automatic pilot...One goal of hypnosis, as well as meditation, is to access the subconscious...In the subconscious mind mental processes occur without our conscious perception of them...The subconscious is not limited by our imposed boundaries of logic, space, and time. It can remember everything, from any time...Afterwards, the person remembers everything experienced during the hypnosis session."[7] Brian Weiss refers to regression therapy as: "...the mental act of going back to an earlier time, whenever that time may be, in order to retrieve memories that may still be negatively influencing a patient's present life and that are probably the source of the patient's symptoms."[8]

Psychologist Dr. Michael Newton has been one of the frontrunners of spiritual regression, a hypnosis therapy whereby the subject goes back to life between lives (i.e. life experiences between two reincarnations), and life after death.

He utilizes a hypnosis whereby the subject reaches deeper theta ranges of hypnosis, rather than the classical alpha range used for general practice. Michael Newton writes: "With the use of deep hypnosis I have the advantage as a spiritual regressionist of utilizing both the soul mind and current human ego. The superconscious mind operates within an eternal framework which the subconscious is able to process into current reality."[9]

In the forty years that Michael Newton has practiced, he has come to revelatory information from his subjects on what happens when we die and rebirth. He explains that it did not matter which (non) religious background a person had, once the person was under hypnosis, they were consistent in their reports. None of his subjects in his decades of practice has ever encountered a major religious figure during a séance. None of his subjects has ever encountered the "seven planes of existence" as noted in Eastern spiritual philosophy. None of his subjects has ever been possessed by another spirit, or heard of such phenomena. None of his subjects ever was a "twin soul", as no soul seems alike.[10] "Still, the prophets of all the major religions are reflections of God to their followers. I feel the acceptance of prophets in many religions around the world has its roots in our soul memory of sacred intermediaries – such as guides and Elders – between ourselves and the creator Source."[11]

Psychic Sylvia Browne has been doing similar work as Michael Newton for over three decades, combining regressive hypnosis with her psychic abilities. During hypnosis and psychic counseling of her patients over the years, Browne has reached very similar conclusions as Newton has on reincarnation, "life between lives", and the Ultimate Reality. Through her foundation she has been able to document, trace and proof the existence of past lives. The foundation has gathered thousands of confirmed cases.[12] Sylvia Browne writes that curses do not exist. She never encountered one of her thousands of patients and clients that had been cursed. Neither has she encountered clients who could not or would not be hypnotized. All of her clients visit at least one past-life during a session. She explains the conventional "seven levels" of Eastern religion as advancement categories in the Ultimate Reality.[13]

Brian Weis: "High school dropouts, nuclear physicists, attorneys, and professional athletes all tell me virtually the same things about the spiritual state and our purpose on this earth. This lends considerable credence to their experiences. Once more I want to emphasize that these findings are clinical, accumulated from hundreds of patients. Finding so much similarity and so many correlations is highly significant statistically."[14]

Michael Newton speaks of our soul as an intelligent form of light energy that travels after death to another dimension called the spirit world or Ultimate Reality, comparable with our modern notion of heaven. He explains that each soul has his own "fingerprint" and unique identity, composition and rate of vibration.[15] It can take many years for a soul to adjust his own vibrations with the of a host brain.[16]

Hypnotized patients of Weiss claim that it is abnormal to be in a physical state, compared to the natural spiritual state.[17] Apparently when in spiritual form there is a strong sense of happiness and well-being.[18]

A soul seems to join the mother's womb sometime after the third month of pregnancy. After birth, Michael Newton describes, an amnesiac memory block sets in. Newton has never encountered a case whereby the soul joined the fetus in the first trimester. Some of his subjects have "talked to their body as a second entity up to the age of six".[19]

Quiet contemplation, sleep, meditation and hypnosis can provide a method of contact with the Ultimate Reality and a method to connect with our subconscious. There seem to be a connection between heaven and earth though the means of thought-waves. Apparently communication between souls in the Ultimate Reality occurs via telepathy. A dream state also provides access of departed souls or guides to reach people on earth.

The Australian Aborigines believe that dream time is the real time in terms of objective reality.[20]

Because children have not been conditioned to doubt or resist the supernatural, they are more receptive to spirits.[21] Sylvia Browne writes the same about the psychic abilities of children.[22]

What Happens in the Brain
Each of the three zones of the triune brain (brainstem, limbic system, cerebral cortex) has its own storehouse for consciousness and memory. The three zones or levels of the brain develop chronologically in the fetus and newborn just as they did in human evolution.[23]

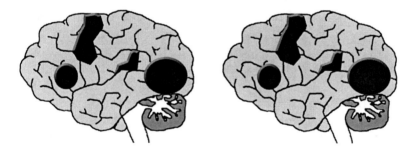

Brain areas most active during hypnosis (black)

Janov writes: "A trance state occurs when the person operates from the first (brainstem) and second (limbic system) level of consciousness without the benefit of the third level of critical intellect (cerebral cortex). In this state, no cognition is employed to determine whether internal and external conditions coincide, whether how one feels and acts is reality based. Key structures in the limbic-emotional system mediate in what occurs in both hypnosis and in the neurotic trance. The limbic structures amygdala and the hippocampus are involved in making feelings conscious and in making feelings repressed and unconscious – dissociating feelings from acknowledgment. The hippocampus can retrieve emotions and with the help of the thalamus can keep them out of consciousness. It is what accomplishes entrance into the hypnotic state; the limbic hippocampus is heavily responsible for the disconnection from conscious awareness. The amygdala can activate emotions and can keep current input from triggering off those emotions. The thalamus and basal ganglia help by refusing to relay certain information from below to higher levels. In that way, too, we remain dissociated."[24]

Janov explains that there is yet another system that keeps us alert and consciously vigilant, and that is the reticular activating system of the brain stem (RAS). If that system is blocked we are less alert and critical. In the lulled, parasympathetic state of a beginning trance, it is that alerting system that goes off service. Janov continues to explain that: "It is primarily the limbic system, where the emotional level of consciousness is organized, that "decides" whether to make a feeling fully conscious. It is here that dissociation can take place. It is here that the rhythms of the brain can be slowed down into the theta (slow) rhythms indicating the predominance of a lower or second line level of consciousness at work. Here is where the input from the hypnotist enters and is accepted unquestioningly. As the brain rhythms slow even more into the delta range, down to 2 or 3 cycles per second, the person can enter a deep trance where even suggestion no longer enters. She is "out," no longer in this world; she is rigid and unyielding. She is operating on the first-line only, where survival functions dominate. The left hemisphere of the brain, with its severely diminished activity, is now practically useless. There is no critical capacity whatsoever. Attention is narrowed only to the voice of the hypnotist and what he is suggesting, and even that is at a minimal level."[25]

John Gruzelier, a psychologist at Imperial College in London used fMRI scans on 12 subjects that were highly susceptible to hypnosis and 12 with low susceptibility. According to Anna Gossline's article on his research: "Under hypnosis, Gruzelier found that the highly susceptible subjects showed significantly more brain activity in the anterior cingulate gyrus than the weakly susceptible subjects. This area of the brain has been shown to respond to errors and evaluate emotional outcomes. The highly susceptible group also showed much greater brain activity on the left side of the prefrontal cortex than the weakly susceptible group. This is an area involved with higher level cognitive processing and behaviour."[26]

Research by Faymonville et al. used PET scans of hypnotized subjects to show activity in the anterior cingulate cortex (midcingulate area 24a'). Faymonville et al., conclude in that there is activity increase between the cingulated cortex (area surrounding the corpus calossum which includes the cingulated gyrus) and the thalamus, brainstem and right prefrontal cortex.[27]

BINAURAL BEAT STIMULATION

Travel Method

There is a (cautious) estimate that two percent of modern adults have an inborn ability to access AESC spontaneously and at will (such as out of body experiences - OBE). If two percent (approximately 130 million people) of every human population throughout history had this same ability, trance-states have provided our ancestors access to other realities and entities.[1]

Research indicates that some 25 percent of our population remembers having at least one AESC experience.[2]

The late Robert A. Monroe has been the first in utilizing binaural beat stimulation to obtain AESC, with as aim obtaining the out of body experience (OBE). The Virginia businessman was able to obtain spontaneous OBE and travel to ODR at will. He encountered many alien intelligent beings during his OBEs. Because of his engineering and radio broadcasting background, Monroe started experimenting with sound to manipulate brainwave frequencies to obtain AESC. He succeeded and founded the Monroe Institute in Faber, Virginia. Several programs can be followed at the institute, whereby participants may obtain AESC and visits to ODRs through binaural beat technology. Thousands of persons have done so since its opening in 1972. In addition to consciousness exploration, the Monroe Institute has done extensive research to the properties of binaural beat technology to aid in meditation, relaxation, visualization, sleep, and healing. The institute sells CDs with a variety of these applications online. Since its success, many other businesses are offering binaural beat machines, software and CDs.

Robert. A. Monroe describes the sequence of obtaining OBE.

He writes that first a relaxed state is to be obtained, which is often followed by a vibration (with a cycle below 60Hz, and ideally around 27Hz), and then followed by a detachment with the physical body. The beginning stage of detachment, however, is described by Monroe as vibrating from approximately 10Hz to 18Hz, sometimes accompanied by a hissing sound. Going back into the physical body is achieved by the thought process; just thinking about it instantaneously makes it happen.[3] Fear is the main obstacle, which is also the case with the use of psychedelics. Most success to achieve OBE seems when the body is in a North-South alignment with the head North; when people are healthy; and in a warm environment.

John O.M. Bockris writes of research done at the University of Virginia whereby monotonous sine-waves were played in the ears of volunteers. When these volunteers were asked to imagine that they had left their bodies, 42% stated they did. The EEG of these volunteers showed that theta waves were predominant during the activity, which is similar as during AESC states achieved during meditation, prayer, spiritual regression hypnosis and certain psychedelic use.[4]

Bockris also analyses the work of Robert Monroe who obtained OBE's with his volunteers by use of binaural beat technology. According to Bockris, in the OBE state one is in a plastic parallel of the real world which alters when we physically alter ourselves.[5]

Bockris also reports that there is a remarkable consistency about how these higher worlds manifest according to research performed by Monroe and other researchers in this field, such as Callaway, Forham and Fox. OBE volunteers apparently speak of three different worlds they may encounter. The first one being similar to our own; the second one being of great beauty, which at times shows spirits of deceased; and occasionally a third world is seen, which seems to be an older version of our world.[6]

Rosalind A. McKnight, one of Robert Monroe's first and

foremost "test explorers" on his binaural beat programs, outlines that there are several levels in which our consciousness (soul) exists. Within five dimensions of the human self, there are seven levels of energy, according to McKnight, also called the seven charkas.[7] The Monroe Institute identifies the different levels of AESC as Focus levels. Dreaming is considered an energy cleansing process going through all five levels during sleep. Focus 23, 24-26, 27, and beyond unto 34 and 35 are advanced focus areas, which are all above level 4, in which individual information and direct experience can be obtained.

What Happens in the Brain

In 1839 a German by the name of H.W. Dove discovered binaural beats. Binaural beats are signals of two different, but nearly similar, audio frequencies (sounds) that are separately presented to a different ear of the same person. To do this, stereo headphones or stereo speakers are used. The brain interprets these different signals by creating a "binaural beat" (phantom signal) that equals the difference in frequency between the two original frequencies.

For example, if the left hear is exposed to a sound of 200 Hz and the right ear to a sound of 205 Hz, the brain creates a binaural beat of 205-200 = 5 Hz. Even though the binaural beat cannot be heard by the ear (the human range of hearing is from 20 to 20,000 Hz), it is nevertheless perceived as an auditory beat in the brain.

When the brain starts to resonate with this binaural beat, it thus "follows" it. This "FFR" or frequency following response has been named and researched in 1973 by Gerald Oster of the Mount Sinai Hospital in New York City. This FFR response to auditory stimuli, whereby the brain entrains to or resonates at the frequency of an external stimulus, can be recorded at the top of the head (vertex of the brain) with any EEG-recording machine.

Whole brain synchronization (or hemispheric synchronization) is when at one point both hemispheres of the brain start to resonate (entrain) together to a binaural beat. Hemispheric synchronization is a pre-requisite for AESC. This synchronization is also evident in advanced meditators.

The 200 Hz and 205 Hz in the above example are referred to as "carrier frequencies". By lowering the carrier frequencies, to for example 190 Hz and 195 Hz, the brain receives an extra push according to Bill Harris. He continues to analyze that with this extra push, the hemispheric synchronization process becomes more powerful. He warns however at an instant introduction of ultra low carrier frequencies. His experience with very low carrier frequencies introduced too fast was that the brain over-produces certain neurochemicals resulting in a few days of euphoria followed by a mental, emotional and physical freak out.[8]

Using carrier sounds of less then 1000 Hz is recommendable to create binaural beats in the head, as the wave length signal below 1000 Hz is longer then the diameter of the human skull. The full sound wave then curves around the head by diffraction and is heard by both ears. But since it curves around the head, one ear hears the sound a fraction before the other ear hears and interprets it. The brain interprets these signals as "out of phase" with each other. Because of this ability to hear out of phase signals, the brain is able to perceive binaural beats.[9]

Research was conducted on the Gateway Voyage of the Monroe Institute in a group setting. The Gateway Voyage is a program whereby binaural beat technology masked with brown noise (verbal guidance) or pink noise (music or background sounds) aims to achieve the AESC and out of body experiences. Todd J. Masluk examined these AESC and related peak experiences of 160 participants of the program. The research concluded that peak experiences (72%) occurred with regularity during the Gateway Voyage program while participants were listening to tapes with binaural beat technology, which induced hemispheric synchronization.[10] Masluk concludes in writing: "This great variety and depth of experiences suggest that Gateway helps to facilitate a huge opening or expansion of consciousness. This expansion seems to occur in both the outer and inner dimensions of being. Interestingly, the types, intensity and richness of patterns of experience reported bear a striking resemblance to those reported by psychedelic (LSD) researchers. One becomes more physically, mentally, emotionally, and spiritually awake."[11]

The induction of theta-frequency binaural beat technology increased the hypnotic susceptibility in otherwise low susceptible participants.[12]

Because binaural beats can alter the electrochemical environment of the brain, different altered states can be experienced. It is also referred to as the "mind awake / body asleep" state induced by binaural beats, whereby a unique state of consciousness emerges when brainwaves move to lower frequencies while the person maintains awareness.[13]

Monroe writes that participants ("explorers") of sessions at the Monroe Institute underwent a change in body voltage and other biomonitoring data once they reached Focus 12 and interacted / communicated with other intelligent entities.[14] Furthermore he identifies "delta" sleep as the point where consciousness detaches from our physical state whereby the body operates autonomous and can recall consciousness when needed.[15]

Monroe describes that the left brain can be considered as the mind modified by the human body; and the right brain as our core-self, our original energy, untouched by the human body. Both are to work closely together on earth. He describes a broad field of energy called "M" which is used to communicate non-verbally. Love and emotions, for example, are described as M adjacent to thought. Animals are more aware of M radiation then humans. Human- generated M fields can be responsible for a person's physical health, healing, curing and even its DNA format.[16]

Because neural activity is electrochemical and brain waves are electromagnetic, brain functions can be modified by altering this environment through use of chemicals, electromagnetic manipulation, or resonant entrainment techniques such as binaural beats. The binaural beat can be used to entrain specific neural rhythms through the FFR, which can be measured and verified. Consciousness cannot be measured with instruments, but indirectly the electro-neurological activity related to consciousness states can. The measured EEG frequencies (op the top of the head) indicate to researchers the estimate state of consciousness. The dominant brainwave signal measurable is a likely indicator of this state.

Binaural beats originate in the brainstem's superior olivary nucleus (see also Appendix I – Brain Stem). This is the area in the brain where auditory sensation is neurologically conveyed to the RAS (reticular activating system located in the brainstem, see also Chapter 6. Appendix I) and hence carried out to the cortex where its EEG brainwaves frequencies can be measured as a result of the frequency following response.

Binaural beats made measurable changes in brainwaves compared to non-significant changes during the placebo stimuli. Brainwave frequencies apparently correspond to the binaural beat frequencies the subjects listened to. The different states of consciousness are regulated by the brain.[17]

Julian Jaynes wrote that the RAS (reticular activating system as discussed in Appendix I), is one of the oldest parts of the nervous system that may not necessarily be related to consciousness, and that it is too common to translate psychological phenomena into neuro-anatomy and chemistry.[18] On the contrary, Atwater's research 20 years later attests that RAS has a profound influence on consciousness states.

Dr. Stuart W. Twemlow performed scientific research and tests on Robert A. Monroe while he underwent self-induced OBE. He concluded that Monroe's brain during OBE was mainly in the Theta state, remaining in a frequency around 5 Hz, never exceeding 10 Hz. Variations in frequency were extremely low, and were equal in the right versus left hemisphere. However the variation was much less on the right side of the brain compared to the left side. He concluded that Monroe was able to focus his consciousness so that his brain power remained in a very narrow frequency band.[19]

States of consciousness are not represented by one single brain wave, but by various different mixing wave forms.[20] Because the brain is divided horizontally (into hemispheres), vertically (brainstem to cerebellum), and functionally (different lobes), Atwater argues that each state of consciousness is interfaced with a different part of the brain, resonating at a specific brain wave frequency in that particular area, whereby the overall state reflects the dominant frequency at the time.

Hemispheric synchronization are associated with meditation and AESC, and are further enhanced and improved upon by the induction of binaural beats of certain low frequencies if these are complex frequencies (mimicking brain waves) instead of single standing frequencies (standing sine waves).

Brain functions and related brainwaves can be altered through entrainment of the FFR with binaural beat technology, resulting in hemispheric synchronization. However, consciousness alterations induced by binaural beats seem to follow a distinct route independent from entrainment. In order to alter consciousness it is necessary to provide some sort of information input to the RAS, and that binaural beats seem to provide this consciousness-altering information. The RAS in turn alters arousal states, attention-focus and levels of awareness. [21]

Binaural beats mimicking complex brain wave frequencies (and measurable by EEG FFR) are recognized by RAS as brain wave pattern information. He goes on to state that if this information is not conflicted by internal stimuli (such as fear) and external stimuli (such as noise), the RAS will alter the state of consciousness as a natural function by regulating brain activity while integrating the binaural beat stimulus as if it was a natural function. It can be stated that binaural beats influence two different processes (via entrainment of the FFR with as result hemispheric synchronization *and* via RAS with as result alteration of elements of consciousness), with as combined result AESC. As evidence to his, there are various studies whereby measurable changes in RAS function and in cortical EEG (which is regulated by RAS) during exposure to binaural beats were evident.[22]

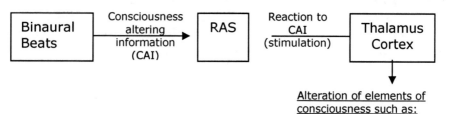

| Binaural Beats | Consciousness altering information (CAI) → | RAS | Reaction to CAI (stimulation) | Thalamus Cortex |

Alteration of elements of consciousness such as:
- arousal states
- attention/focus
- levels of awareness

Table 15 - Consciousness and binaural beats

Listening to binaural beats through stereo headphones may bring the listener into AESC if the listener is a willing participant to the exercise. Passive listening to binaural beats may not necessarily have any effect on one's states of consciousness, therefore the participant is encouraged to be prepared and relaxed. AESC may be facilitated by utilizing music, verbal guidance, breathing exercises, humming, biofeedback and relaxation techniques in addition to the binaural beats.

Alpha-frequency binaural beat stimulation increased alpha brain production. However, it could not be concluded that this was solely due to a FFR, since the participants also received relaxation response instructions. Another group in the study listened only to surf sounds of the ocean with the same relaxation response instructions. Alpha brain production also increased in this group.[23]

Personal exploration of AESC achievable with the use of this technology include and are not limited to (deep) meditation, hypnagogic states, intuition development, remote viewing and out of body experiences, depending on the frequencies induced through binaural beats and on the intensity of user participation. Even though binaural beat technology has a direct effect on brain wave activity and cortical arousal, induction of binaural beat technology by itself is no guarantee for success in AESC. In order to have an enhanced possibility of success (and avoiding falling asleep) in achieving and exploring expanded states with the use of binaural beat technology, it is strongly suggested to be well prepared. Preparation includes a willingness and motivation to participate; relaxation of body and mind prior to commencement; calm and comfortable environment; getting into a physically comfortable position; letting go of fear; use of proper equipment to listen to binaural beats.

REPETITIVE & RHYTHMIC STIMULATION

Travel Method

Any combination of rhythm (song, clapping, music, speaking in tongues) accompanied by ongoing repetitive movements (dance, flagellation, swirling) can be methods to achieve AESC in many known rituals around the world.

One of the examples of use of repetitive body movements accompanied by rhythmic drumming to induce AESC is the trance-dance of the Bushman, also called San or Basarwa, of the Kalahari Desert (Namibia, South Africa, and Botswana). This grueling form of circular dance can last up to 24 hours whereby shamans (!gi:ten) undertake voyages to other realities during AESC.

The Bradshaw Foundation's website states: "Dancers stomp in a circle around the campfire for many hours. The women clap the rhythm of the circular dance and sing powerful songs. After hours of stomping, some dancers start to slip into trance or half-trance. In this AESC many have out-of-body experiences. They describe traveling to the spirit realm. Those dancers who practice and utilize OBE on a regular basis are termed shamans. Up to 40% of the members of any one group may be practicing shamans."[1]

The Metropolitan Museum of Art's website states: "The rhythmic singing and clapping and the intense dancing for hours on end produce altered states of consciousness in which the shamans experience, first, visual imagery, and later, more complex multi sensory hallucinations. To call these experiences "hallucinations" is, of course, to look at them from a detached Western academic perspective; for the San, these experiences are deeply moving and profound revelations of a religious reality beyond this world. In order to experience these revelations, they believe that one must harness the supernatural energy from the dead animal. This energy enters the body, where it "boils" in the stomach, forcing it to rise into the heads of the dancers, where it explodes, catapulting them into the other world."[2]

The ODRs visited during AESC incurred due to repetitive and rhythmic stimulation seem to depend on the depth of the trance during the exercise. Well seasoned voyagers in this mode of travel bring back stories of the Geometric ODR, Hybrid ODR and occasionally also the Humanoid ODR.

The Bushmen portray the voyages of their shamans in rock art. These rock art depictions are similar as those of Upper Paleolithic cave art, with the same themes. Bleeding noses are seen on these type of African rock art as stemming from a dancing man or therianthrope.

The shaman's nose bleeding occurs frequently during circular trance-dances once he enters an AESC. The physical cause of this phenomenon is dehydration and subsequent hemorrhage

of fragile nose vessels. The bushmen-shaman obtains a variety of information from the "other side" related to healing, hunting and the weather. Often they undergo painful abuse (similar to those described by psychedelic induced AESC) in return for knowledge. The whole experience is described as an OBE.[3]

Bushmen cave art on sandstone at Ladybrand, near Maseru, Capital of Lesotho, South Africa. Notice the bleeding nose on the figure at right.

More artwork in the same cave at Ladybrand depicts a large trance-dance ritual. Researcher Maarten van Hoek writes that this depicted ritual at Ladybrand show some interesting details, such as: "Women clapping with splayed hands; a squatted figure that may have a nasal bleeding; and a shaman (12 cm in length) who seems to be floating during trance; all the five shamans are bending over and have to use sticks to be able to continue their trance dance; the shamans are wearing shamans' eared caps; a much larger human figure seems to be bending over with his hands raised to the nose, indication of a possible nasal bleeding. This figure has been painted over with the clearer and smaller figures. This may indicate a lapse in time, but equally it may point to an intentional addition to a similar graphic statement."[4]

Cave art stemming from the late stone age at Cederberg Mountains, Bushmans Kloof, South Africa also shows a depiction of a man bleeding profusely from the nose.

Shamanic AESC typically involve singing, changing, drumming, dancing followed by the collapse and apparent consciousness.[5] When persons participate in rhythmic repetitious group rituals, their affective, perceptual, cognitive, and motor processes synchronize within themselves and among the group.[6]

Glossolalia, or "speaking in tongues", is a practice that is utilized by many shamanic tribes throughout the world.[7] Glossolalia is often instigated by gospel singing and music; or it can be initiated by silent, repetitive prayer. Henceforth, an altered state is in which some persons spontaneously speak in tongues. The Pentecostal movement also exercises glossolalia in their faith.

There seems to be no linguistic evidence that a form of language is being spoken during glossolalia. Instead, phonetic sounds are loosely strung together and repeated.[8] Nevertheless, some ministers and shamans interpret and translate glossolalia.

Brian Weiss writes that as a young boy while visiting a Jewish temple each Saturday, he observed the old men sway and rock while reciting and repeating the same prayers. This brought them into an AESC, similar to Weiss bringing his patients under hypnosis. He writes that it was the ritual that brought AESC to these praying men in the temple.[9]

What Happens in the Brain

Even though not all rituals are religious, they all contain elements of rhythm and repetition, and they aim to define the individual as part of some larger group or cause. They outline that slow rhythmic ritual and/or repetitive auditory or visual stimuli can cause AESC. However, if AESC is combined with a state of arousal (due to hyperventilation, dancing, action, and even smells) both states together result in so-called "religious awe". The combination of activating both the parasympathetic (calm) and sympathetic (arousal) creates an intense spiritual experience.[10] Autonomic activity alone seems not sufficient to produce the intense emotional states experienced during ritual.[11]

The sympathetic system of arousal project from the amygdale to the left hemisphere (analytical, rational); whereas the parasympathetic system of relaxation project from the septum to the right hemisphere (integrative, holistic).[12]

Repetitive drumbeats at the rate of 4.5 Hz for example, can induce the theta brainwave state. Brain wave patterns corresponding to AESC due to singing, drumming and dancing are in the theta and low alpha range.[13]

Michael Winkelman writes about AESC induced by shamans: "The overall physiological dynamics involve an activation of the sympathetic division of the autonomic nervous through drumming and dancing until exhaustion of the sympathetic system from extreme exertion leads to collapse into a parasympathetic dominant state characterized by the relaxation response and intense visual activity. This same stimulation and collapse cycle is produced by many other procedures, including: fasting, sleeping and dreaming, hallucinogenic drugs. Sometimes shamans enter this phase of relaxation AESC directly through withdrawal and an internal focus of attention, rather than extensive induction procedures and the sympathetic system stimulation...The overall effect of the shamanic AESC is to dominate the frontal part of the brain with information from the emotional and behavioral brains."[14]   He continues: "These shamanic activities that stimulate release of the body's own opioid system include: exhaustive rhythmic physical activities (e.g., dancing and clapping); exposure to temperature extremes (e.g., cold or sweat lodges); and austerities such as prolonged water deprivation and fasting, flagellation, and self inflicted wounds. Opiods are also elicited by emotional manipulations involving fear and positive expectations, as well as the nighttime activities typical of shamanic ritual, when endogenous opioids are naturally highest...Activation of the opioid system also produces a sense of euphoria, certainty and belongingness."[15]

Andrew Newberg, Eugene d'Aguili and Vince Rause write that: "Research reveals that repetitive rhythmic stimulation, like the mesmerizing call of the wolves, can drive the limbic and autonomic systems, which may eventually alter some very fundamental aspects of the way the brain thinks, feels, and interprets reality. These rhythms can drastically affect the brain's neurological ability to define the limits of the self."[16]

Repetitive, rhythmic stimulations result in a high degree of limbic arousal. They continue to state that the major goal of ritualized behavior is the blending of the self into some larger reality.

The hippocampus helps to link the intentions behind verbal and vocal signals to suitable arousal and emotional states via the amygdale and hypothalamus. Rhythm and sequencing of sounds (dance, chants) stimulate the hippocampus; and that stimulation of the hippocampus may create supernatural experiences by the induction of physically activated trance-states.[17]

There is an important sequence to note though, stimulation occurs first in the temporal lobe → onward to the amygdale and hippocampus → which may result in supernatural experiences. He further writes that during physically induced trance the hippocampus may go into overdrive, because when the hypothalamus gets stimulated, it elicits the expression of emotions. These emotions gain significance by being projected to the amygdale. As a result of the overdrive, he writes, the regular channels of neural transmissions are thrown out of balance. This is backed up by SPECT brain-imaging.

When comparing brain scans of persons speaking in tongues with those of nuns and Buddhist monks, they concluded that the language areas of the frontal lobes were not activated. This in contrast with reading-praying nuns.[18] This proposes that the glossolalia is being produced differently, or possibly away from the normal processing centers of speech.[19]

Also parietal lobe activity did not decrease, as it did with nuns and Buddhist monks, therefore the glossolalia practitioners did not loose their personal sense of self (as did the nuns and monks, which felt union with The Divine and the universe). Nuns, monks and glossolalia practitioners did have increased thalamus activity, making their spiritual experiences feel real.

Apparently the suspension of one's will is required when a person exhibits involuntary behaviors during certain rituals, such as spirit possession, Ouija board spelling, dousing, or hypnosis. Because frontal lobe activity is decreased, one has the conscious feeling that an outer entity is in charge.[20] When frontal lobe activities are halted, memory functions decrease, whereby the brain can transform strange sounds into words and phrases when it hears certain musical or noise patterns (such as happens when listening to glossolalia).[21]

Meaning that is given to these glossolalia utterances is closely connected to the social and cultural belief system of the group. Speaking in tongues seems fundamentally different from the spiritual experiences obtained through prayer and meditation.[22]

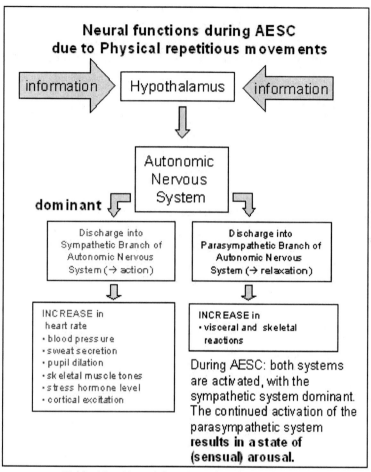

Table 16 – Neural functions during AESC due to
Physical repetitious movements

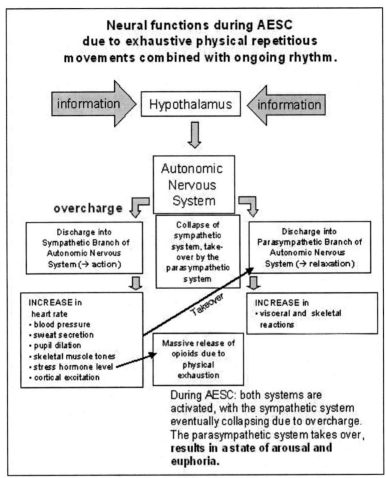

Table 17 – Neural functions during AESC due to exhaustive physical repetitious movements combined with ongoing rhythm

ELECTRIC & ELECTRO-MAGNETIC STIMULATION

Travel Method
The work of Dr. Michael A. Persinger (Neuropsychologist and Head of the Neuroscience Laboratory at Laurentian University in Sudbury, Ontario) shows that electromagnetic fields seem to interact with the human brain to trigger AESC states. The laboratory volunteers of Persinger's research received weak electromagnetic currents directed at certain locations in the brain through so-called solenoid head sets. These are electromagnetic field generators that are arranged around a person's head directed at the temporal lobe and parietal lobe areas. Subjects with excitable temporal lobes have more pronounced effects.[1]

ODRs visited during this travel method range from the Geometric, Hybrid and Humanoid ODR to the Shadow ODR. The latter may include unpleasant experiences. The Ultimate Reality and a visit to The Divine are also frequently mentioned by those using electric and electro-magnetically induced AESC.

Dr. Michael Persinger started his research nearly four decades ago. He used low intensity magnetic fields applied to certain areas of the scalp, in a technique called TMS (transcranial magnetic stimulation). These fields also occur naturally due to geomagnetic or electromagnetic factors.[2]

Persinger used magnetic fields of 1 uT (micro Tesla), which is smaller compared to the earth's magnetic field of 50 micro Tesla. The induction of this small magnetic field in the brain creates an electrical current, which in turn affects certain areas in the brain, and hence their functions. One Tesla is a unit of magnetic flux density. MRI (Magnetic Resonance Imaging) machines in hospitals are calibrated in Tesla units, in the range of ½ T to 6 T.[3] A magnetometer can provide measurements of magnetic fields.

Magnetic Field Strength in T (Tesla)	
1 nT = 1 nano Tesla	10^{-9} T
1 uT = 1 micro Tesla	10^{-6} T = 0.000001 Tesla
1 mili Tesla	10^{-3} T = 0.001 T = 1/1000 Tesla
Persinger's TMS research	1 uT
Interstellar space	10 nT
Earth's magnetic field	50 uT
Geomagnetic fields GMF	10-100 uT
Electromagnetic fields EMF	100-500 uT (micro Tesla)
Small bar magnet	0.01 Tesla
Big electromagnet	1½ Tesla
MRI scanning machine	½-6 Tesla
Strong lab magnet	10 Tesla

Table 18 – Tesla, unit of magnetic flux density

Both temporal lobes and parietal lobes induced by electromagnetic pulses were following a burst-firing pattern, whereby certain frequency pulses were brought on every several seconds or so for a period of several minutes. Sometimes these were combined by first inducing a continuous bilateral frequency modulated field for several minutes, following by the burst-firing pattern. It seems that about 80% of participants following these two patterns of electromagnetic induction reported the feeling of a presence. Apparently the most effective configuration included burst-firings of 3 mili seconds. Michael A. Persinger writes: "If the presence occurs during the right hemispheric stimulation, the experience appears to be along the left side and to be more emotional (or fearful, including ghosts or demons, devils, etc.). If the experience does not occur until the bilateral stimulation, the location of the "being" is perceived to be more right or on both sides and to be pleasant, even spiritual."[4] "We have also found that the sensed presence whose attributions range from bereavement apparitions to visitations from Gods or aliens, occurs more frequently between midnight and 06 hr local time, and in particular between 02 hrs and 04 hrs local time. This peak is the same period in which the greatest proportion of overt displays of temporal lobe seizures were recorded during the late nineteenth century before the implementation of effective medications."[5]

"If one could extract from the brain the essential electromagnetic structure with which the experience of God is correlated and then re-apply this pattern to the person's brain without their knowledge, would that person experience God?"[6]

Persinger's hypothesis states that the sensed presence is the prototype of the God experience (right hemisphere) compared to the sense of self (left hemisphere). He states that the most common descriptions of the "sensed presence" include such experiences of body-vibrations, dreamlike states, out of body experience (OBE), spinning, fear, aggression or sexual arousal. During his 15 years of research, Persinger concludes that these experiences undergone by students, journalists, older people and artists alike, seem to reflect their (cultural) belief systems. As example he writes that when magnetic fields were applied over the right hemisphere of participants in a laboratory setting, God or religious entities that were experienced correlated with the person's belief. Atheists who participated in the experiences also noted sensed presences or reported an out of body experience, but attribute these to their own cognitive processes. Therefore Persinger concludes that the feeling of a presence is a property of the human brain and human experience.

What Happens in the Brain
Author and contributing editor to The New York Times Magazine, Harper's and This American Life Jack Hitt describes Persinger's research as follows: "When the right hemisphere of the brain, the seat of emotion, is stimulated in the cerebral region presumed to control notions of the self, and then the left hemisphere, the seat of language, is called upon to make sense of this nonexistent entity, the mind generates a "sensed presence."[7]

John O.M. Bockris summarizes: "Persinger in 1989 has developed the concept of the limbic system and in particular the right temporal lobe and associated lobe structures as the center of spiritual activity."[8] "Thus, low electric currents to the right temporal lobe produces feelings, some of which correspond to those of heightened religious experience."[9]

Andrew Newberg and, Eugene d'Aguili describe: "Electrical stimulation of limbic structures in human subjects produces dreamlike hallucinations, out-of-body sensations, déjà vu, and illusions, all of which have been reported to spiritual states. The primary structures of the limbic system are the hypothalamus, the amygdale, and the hippocampus. All are primitive organs, but their influence upon the human mind is considerable."[10]

Persinger's research indicates that persons with excitable temporal lobes (those with for example a particular temporal lobe epilepsy) report significantly more "sensed presences" than those persons who have low temporal lobe lability when using magnetic fields with a strength of approximately 1 uT. In 75% compared to 60%, the presences were more felt when TMS was applied to the right hemisphere of the brain compared to application to both hemispheres. Even application of weaker electromagnetic fields still resulted in some persons with high temporal lobe lability sensing a presence. Therefore Persinger concluded that haunt phenomena can be related to natural forces stimulating certain brain areas.[11]

Laurence O. McKinney writes of research, whereby electrodes were implanted in the hippocampus of rats. These rats had a button which they could touch to activate the electrodes. The rats would activate the buttons until they dropped from exhaustion. The apparent pleasure perceived by activation of their hippocampus, was preferred by the rats over sex or food.[12] He also argues that: "If the hippocampus is over-stimulated too long, its cellular mechanisms will start to fault down."[13] "If this happens, our virtual reality, our sense of the world and its meaning will destabilize."[14]
As the limbic system provides the boundaries between thought and belief and chronological time, McKinney argues, its

distortion provides altered perceptions of dreams, delusions, and death.

Rhawn Joseph lists research done with direct depth electrode activation of the amygdale, which can evoke memories of sexual intercourse and traumatic memories that had long been forgotten. He writes that direct electrical stimulation of the temporal lobes, hippocampus and amygdale results in the recollection of images, as well as the creation of fully formed visual and auditory hallucination.[15] "..that stimulation of the right amygdale produces complex visual hallucinations, body sensations, deja vus, illusions, as well as gustatory and alimentary experiences. Apparently stimulation of the right hippocampus also produces memory and dream-like hallucinations."[16] "Intense activation of the temporal lobe and amygdale has also been reported to give rise to a host of sexual, religious and spiritual experiences; and chronic hyper stimulation (i.e. seizure activity) can induce some individuals to become hyper-religious or visualize and experience ghosts, demons, angels and even God, as well as claim demonic and angelic possession of or the sensation of having left their body."[17] "Fear and rage reactions have also been triggered in humans following depth electrode stimulation of the amygdale."[18]

It is the amygdale that makes it possible to feel moody, and generates feelings of fear. He further writes in the same chapter that the abnormal amygdale activity, or amygdale, can alter sex drive and sexual orientation, and can also induce a loss of social interest. If the amygdale is directly stimulation, rage reactions are commonly triggered, as well as sensations of extreme pleasure and hyper sexuality. Joseph also notes that in the midst of a temporal lobe seizure, patients are known to have attacked people near to them. "Indeed, the amygdale is able to overwhelm the neocortex and the rest of the brain, so that the person not only forms religious ideas, but responds to them, sometimes with vicious, horrifying results."[19]

Joseph also writes that sex and food along with fear, rage and aggression, and religious experiences are probably the most powerful of all limbic emotions (hypothalamus, amygdale, temporal and frontal lobes). He continues that under conditions of extreme fear or emotional trauma, the brain secretes many stress hormones and neurochemicals (corticosteroids, encephalin, norepinephrine, serotonin, dopamine), which' fluctuations in turn negatively impact the amygdala and hippocampus. For example, the hippocampus may weaken and the amygdale may become overly activated. Joseph explains this NDE or OBE phenomenon as where the hippocampus is transposing and hallucinating one's image. Because of the massive release of opiates, he writes, loss of fear and the experience of tranquility and joy occur at the same time. He writes: "In fact, it has been repeatedly demonstrated that hyper activation or electrical stimulation of the inferior temporal lobe and amygdale-hippocampal complex can cause some individuals to report they have left their bodies and are hovering upon the ceiling staring down."[20]

Researchers from the University Hospitals of Geneva and Lausanne (Switzerland) have found that OBEs can be produced by direct electrical stimulation of a specific part of the brain. Dr. Olaf Blanke and his colleagues at the Federal Polytechnic School of Lausanne worked with a 43-year-old female patient who suffered from right temporal lobe epilepsy. In order to identify the location where the seizures occurred, the researchers implanted electrodes on the brain under the patient's dura (outermost of the three layers surrounding the protective membrane of the brain and spinal cord). While the patient was awake, the researchers could pass electrical current through the electrodes to identify the function of the brain area under each electrode. Electrical stimulation of the angular gyrus on the right side of the patient's brain produced unusual sensations. Weak stimulation caused the patient to feel as if she was "sinking into the bed" or "falling from a height." Stronger electrical stimulation caused the patient to have an OBE. For example, the patient said, "I see myself lying in bed, from above, but I only see my legs and lower trunk." Stimulation of the angular gyrus at other times caused the woman to have feelings of "lightness" and of "floating" two meters above the bed. The angular gyrus is located near the vestibular (balance) area of the cerebral cortex. It is likely that electrical stimulation of the angular gyrus interrupts the ability of the brain to make sense of information related to balance and touch. This interruption may result in OBEs. Blood flow changes within the angular gyrus may alter brain activity during "near death experiences." This may result in OBEs reported by people who survive such events.[21]

One Body When the Brain Says Two

A recent study conducted by Dr. Olaf Blanke provides new scientific insight into experiences more often left to paranormal explanations. Stimulating a part of the brain called the angular gyrus on opposing sides yielded two distinct results:

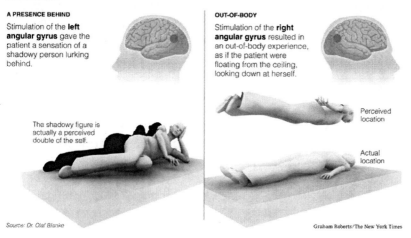

A PRESENCE BEHIND

Stimulation of the **left angular gyrus** gave the patient a sensation of a shadowy person lurking behind.

The shadowy figure is actually a perceived double of the self.

OUT-OF-BODY

Stimulation of the **right angular gyrus** resulted in an out-of-body experience, as if the patient were floating from the ceiling, looking down at herself.

Perceived location

Actual location

Source: Dr. Olaf Blanke

Graham Roberts/The New York Times

Angular gyrus stimulation.
Reprinted with permission of The New York Times and Graham Roberts.

Olaf Blanke and colleagues say their discovery might help shed light on brain processes that contribute to the symptoms of schizophrenia, which can include the sensation that one's own actions are being performed by someone else. Doctors evaluating a woman with no history of psychiatric problems found stimulation of an area of her brain called the left temporo-parietal junction caused her to believe a person was standing behind her (note: the temporo-parietal junction is located between the temporal and parietal lobe).

The patient reported that "person" adopted the same bodily

positions as her, although she didn't recognize the effect as an illusion. At one point in the investigation, the patient was asked to lean forward and clasp her knees: this led to a sensation that the shadow figure was embracing her, which she described as unpleasant. The finding could be a step towards understanding psychiatric affects such as feelings of paranoia, persecution and alien control, say neuroscientists.[22]

Todd Murphey, a Researching Behavioral Scientist associated with Dr. Michael Persinger, writes that when the amygdale is stimulated, a presence is sensed. If the left amygdale is more active, then the experience is pleasant. If the right amygdale is more activated, the experience is unpleasant. Coincidentally, unpleasant feelings where felt to occur on the right side of a person, where the pleasant feelings were felt on the left side. Sometimes images arose of these presences, and were described as: angels, monks in hooded robes, knights, spirits, deities, aliens and another variety.[23]

Rhawn Joseph writes: "Neurosurgical patients have reported communing with spirits or receiving profound knowledge from the Hereafter, following depth electrode amygdale stimulation or activation. Some have reported hearing the singing of angels and the voice of "God".[24] "..perhaps the presence of "God" triggers hyperactivity in the limbic system of those chosen to be His prophets, which thus enables them to hear and see god-like stimuli as well as causing them to demonstrate signs of temporal lobe abnormalities."[25] ".. these limbic structures periodically become hyper activated and open windows and doorways to alternate realities or dimensions which are normally hidden from view."[26]

OTHER MEANS TO TRAVEL

Disease
Studies by Slater and Beard of schizophrenia-like psychoses of epilepsy have found that 38% of these patients had hallucinations and mystical experiences, even though only 9% of these patients had religious convictions prior to the onset of symptoms. Research by Karragulla & Robertson and Geschwind found that typical religious experiences of temporal lobe epileptics include: "greater awareness, seeing Christ come down from the sky, seeing Heaven open, hearing God speak, and believing the patient is God." Loud music, sudden noises and bright light can drive an epileptic into seizures and thoughts of fear and paranoia.[1]

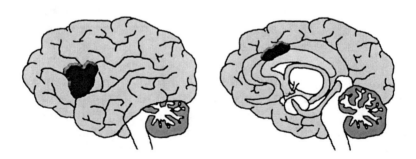

Brain areas most active during a bout of schizophrenia (black).

Of the various psychological diseases known that distort our sense of reality, schizophrenia and temporal lobe epilepsy are the better known. Schizophrenia is a chronic, severe and disabling brain disease.[2]

Melissa K. Spearing writes: "People with schizophrenia often suffer terrifying symptoms such as hearing internal voices not heard by others, or believing that other people are reading their minds, controlling their thoughts, or plotting to harm them. These symptoms may leave them fearful and withdrawn. Their speech and behavior can be so disorganized that they may be incomprehensible or frightening to others. People with schizophrenia may have perceptions of reality that are strikingly different from the reality seen and shared by others around them. Living in a world distorted by hallucinations, illusions and delusions, individuals with schizophrenia may feel frightened, anxious, and confused. Although hallucinations can occur in any sensory form – auditory (sound), visual (sight), tactile (touch), gustatory (taste), and olfactory (smell) – hearing voices that other people do not hear is the most common type of hallucination in schizophrenia."[3]

Temporal lobe epilepsy can be due to head injury, meningitis (brain infection) or unknown causes. Seizures can be barely noted, or can have frightening or pleasurable experiences.[4] Temporal lobe epilepsy results from an electrical disturbance in the brain, often followed by episodes that can vary from blinking eyes, to sudden falls or convulsions.[5] Seizures are the manifestation of abnormal hyper-synchronous discharges of cortical neurons. Temporal lobe epilepsy originates in the medial or lateral temporal lobe.

About 25 percent of patients with temporal lobe epilepsy are obsessed with religion. Dr. Vilayanur Ramashandran explains that patient's seizures caused damage to the pathway that connects two areas of the brain: the one that recognizes sensory information and the one that gives such information emotional context.[6]

Certain combinations of sounds have been shown to trigger epileptic seizures, demonstrating that music has a direct effect on the brain.[7] Experiences similar to those in near death experiences come to epileptics. Researcher Neppe "has found evidence that psychic ability is associated with temporal lobe dysfunction.[8] Seizures of the right temporal lobe are known to produce feelings of gratification, pleasure and know-all.[9]

The most complex forms of hallucinations are associated with tumors located within the most anterior portion of the temporal lobe (the region containing the amygdale and anterior hippocampus). He also states that some individuals suffering from temporal lobe epilepsy report out of body experiences, and lucidity or crystal clear thinking. Many God experiences have occurred during bouts of temporal lobe epilepsy or other disease. The Russian writer and epileptic Fyodor Dostoyevsky (1821-1881), who was known to state that healthy people cannot comprehend the happiness and touch of God of epileptics experience during seconds before an attack.[10]

Hallucinations (by psychotics)	Pure consciousness states (by non-psychotics)
In general, decrease in frontal lobe activity	In general, increase in frontal lobe activity
Feelings of religious grandiosity	Quieting of the mind
Inflated egotistical importance	Loss of pride and ego
If caused by seizures, experiences are consistent and repetitive (same voices, same message)	Experiences vary
Involves usually a single sensory system (sound, vision, feeling)	Involves a rich variety and combination of sensory systems
Experience can be very negative (angry God)	Experience is uplifting and loving
Experience is afterward described as confusing and maybe a trick of the mind. Over time the experience fades.	Experience is afterward described as very real. This sense of realness remains valid over time.

Table 19 – Hallucinations versus Pure consciousness states

Whereas EEG patterns of electrical activity during mystical experiences of non-psychotic individuals is similar to those of during a bout of temporal-lobe epilepsy, there seem to be a clear distinction between the mystical experiences of a person with temporal lobe epilepsy (or a schizophrenic person) compared to those of a non-psychotic person. Research of Stern & Silberweig explains that schizophrenia-like episodes of epilepsy and schizophrenic hallucinations appear to be associated with *decreased* activity in the frontal cortices, lack of awareness of reality, and a disconnection between the self and the supernatural (who is dominant and often gives instructions). This compared to research by Newberg, whereby meditation and prayer seem to be associated with *increased* activity of the frontal cortices (inferior frontal cortex and dorsolateral prefrontical cortex), hyperawareness of reality, and a participation of the self in the supernatural experience. The altruistic abilities of schizophrenic patients are limited compared to non-psychotic persons.[11]

Rhawn Joseph encompasses various research: "If the amygdale (and hippocampus) is injured or abnormally active, the individual may become emotionally abnormal, they may suffer from hallucinations, they may hear voices, and they may have dissociative episodes and feel as they have been "possessed". In some cases of temporal lobe, amygdale, hippocampal abnormality, the alterations in personality are so dramatic, patients may appear to be possessed by demons or suffering from a multiple personality disorder. In fact, in several cases of multiple personality disorder, EEG or blood flow abnormalities involving the temporal lobe have been demonstrated. Compared to other cortical areas, the most complex, vivid hallucinations, including out-of-body dissociative experiences, have their source in the temporal lobe and the hippocampus and amygdale appear to be responsible agents. Hence, under conditions of extreme emotional stress and trauma, the hippocampus, amygdale and temporal lobe may become abnormally active, and victims may experience extreme sensory distortions and hallucinations, including out-of-body phenomenon."[12]

Cotard's syndrome is a cognitive dysfunction due to the damage of the amygdala according to Matthew Alper. A person with this syndrome may feel alienated or dissociated from his body or body parts. Damage to right parietal lobes results in an altered sense of body consciousness.[13] Hallucinations can be triggered by a variety of factors, such as: some types of temporal lobe epilepsy, drugs, illness, physical exhaustion, emotional stress, sensory deprivation.[14] But no matter the source, hallucinations are not at all capable of giving the mind an experience as believable as that of mystical spirituality.[15]

Water, Oxygen, Glucose Deprivation

When the brain is (temporarily) deprived of essential nutrients, such as water, oxygen and glucose, it can ease the transition into AESC. Often these deprivations are paired with repetitious and/or rhythmic stimulation, flagellation or with relaxation techniques. Deprivation of nutrients can also take place non-deliberate at accidents or on the operating table, when OBE and NDE are known to occur. The body's opioid system becomes activated during deprivation of these essential nutrients, which can produce a sense of ecstasy and belonging. Opioids are also released during fear and anxiety.

Examples of water, oxygen and glucose deprivation to obtain AESC are sweat lodges, breathing techniques and extended fasting. Many known religious figures have used one more of these methods, often combined with prayer or self reflection, and have obtained AESC (Siddhartha, Moses, Jesus, Mohammed). Fasting is still a method in many religions to better connect to The Divine (Baha'i, Buddhist, Catholic, Eastern Orthodox, Hindu, Jewish, Mormon, Pagan, Protestant).

The human breath and breathing process have a great deal to do with the transition between the physical and nonphysical dimensions.[16] Hyperventilation during a San circular dance, as well as directed breathing (i.e. belly breathing during yoga and meditation exercises) are means in which AESC can be obtained.

The common "light at the end of the tunnel" symptom of NDE can be attributed to lack of oxygen to the brain's optic nerve, which will under those circumstances flare erratically. Research by Dr. Karl Jansen found that NDE experiences can be precipitated by low oxygen, low blood flow, low blood sugar, temporal lobe epilepsy, etc, all of which release a flood of the neurochemical glutamate, which in turn triggers a flood of ketamine-like brain chemicals, which in turn leads to AESC. Other researchers introduced intravenous injections of 50-100mg of ketamine to volunteers, with resulted in perceived features commonly associated with NDE. Ketamine as a drug, is used in general anesthesia (it suppresses breathing less then most other anesthetics), and is known to cause hallucinations. It is also used as a medicine to combat alcohol and heroin dependency.[17]

In order to function properly, the brain requires 3.3 ml of oxygen for every 100 grams of mass per minute, and a blood glucose level of 80-120 mg per 100 ml. In addition to this, the brain requires the right blood pressure to eliminate waste toxins.[18]

Parts of the hippocampus are very sensitive to brief periods of physical or chemical trauma. If a particular region of the hippocampus called the Sommer's section (also called CA1 region) is deprived of oxygen (hypoxia) or during insufficient blood supply, it exhibits neural loss. Persinger argues that NDE are often associated with either oxygen or glucose deprivation to parts of the limbic system. An example are temporal lobe epileptics who can report intense religious experiences, visual hallucinations and profound beliefs.[19]

Magnetic Field Disturbances
Weak magnetic field disturbances occur naturally due to geomagnetic or electromagnetic factors. Persinger's research indicate that persons with high temporal lobe lability (such as temporal lobe epileptics with certain complex partial seizures) are sensible to these fields, especially if these fields oscillate in sequence with the EEG activity of the person's temporal lobe structures.[20] Persinger writes: "Increases in global geomagnetic activity have been correlated with increases in both the numbers of "apparitions" and visual sensed presences as well as the numbers of epileptic seizures originating from limbic sources. That the brain is responding to the specific pattern and intensity (greater then about 40 nT) of the daily average global geomagnetic perturbations has been verified by the production of seizures in epileptic rats exposed to experimentally generated magnetic fields that precisely duplicated the temporal structure of geomagnetic fields. One of the likely neurochemical mechanisms by which

increases in geomagnetic activity encourages electric lability within the limbic system is the suppression of the nocturnal levels of melatonin. This serotonin-derivative, primarily synthesized within the pineal organ, has dampening effects upon hippocampal electrical activity. Decreases in melatonin levels have been correlated with periods when daily geomagnetic activity increases above 20nT and have been evoked by the nocturnal application of the experimental magnetic fields with slightly larger strengths."[21]

John O.M. Bockris writes: "Recent work by McGillion has thrown light upon possible rational explanations of certain astrological effects. The center of McGillion's argument is the production of melatonin by the pineal gland. The biosynthesis of melatonin depends on enzymes which are sensitive to light and other radiations. Such enzymes are also sensitive to the strength of the Earth's magnetic field. The degree to which a newborn child is exposed to these influences can alter the level of pineal melatonin and hence affect later development. Hence, there would be expected to be an association between the precise time of birth, in which hemisphere the birth occurs, and the degree of geomagnetic activity.[22] Bockris also lists Soviet work on magnetic effects and their effects on living organisms. ELF (extremely low frequencies emitted by an electromagnetic field) influences certain animals. ELF is used by animals to navigate and prey, and influences our circadian rhythms. Very low ELF is also used on a molecular level during chemical, membrane and synaptic processes in the body. Gradients of ELF are measured in Volt per centimeter or meter (V/m or V/cm)."[23]

Architect Stéphane Cardinaux is specialized in geobiology. A Geobiologist studies lay lines and energy fields of areas and homes. Cardinaux is one of its foremost experts and has studied major architectural structures, pyramids, cathedrals and forests. He writes about electromagnetically charged places. These are called "Courant Tellurique" (energy stream or flow coming from the ground) and can be detected through for example dowsing or a very sensitive ELF monitor or Tesla meters. They are usually located at a cross point of various lay lines and are frequently found above underground rivers, and augment in vibration some 150 to 300%. Some of these areas are "Cosmo Tellurique" (energy streaming to and from the sky). Many of these charged areas are found in natural environments, such as forests, mountains, valleys, caves, springs and wells. Especially at these charged energy areas, so-called "Little People" can be observed or sensed writes Cardinaux. These are entities such as elves, dwarfs, gnomes, trolls that can be observed. He describes a parallel plane to ours, which is in our same space, but exists in a different vibration and (thus) time-zone. This time-zone can be compared to a dream world, where time is disjointed. The entities of this plane can remain in a certain state for months or years without movement, to be "awakened" by our presence and interruption. In order to communicate with us, the entities have to align themselves mentally with our "time". Cardinaux explains that with a "sonotest" one can detect an entity. A "sonotest" can be done by moving a sounding tuning-fork over or though the entity. The tuning fork will suddenly change pitch (vibration). Some persons are able to see the entities. Some persons receive information about the exact location of the "charged area" from these entities. The most common smaller entities observed are Dwarfs (± 30 cm), Gnomes (± 60 cm) and Trolls (±110 -140 cm). They can be solitary or in groups. Cardinaux has observed that at certain energy-areas they can be in the hundreds. Besides the smaller ones, there are also bigger entities, which are mostly solitary, and can measure up to 350cm to 700cm. They often resemble Egyptians or Hindu hybrid-divinities in human clothing, of which the face is animal. These seem guardians of specific energetic areas, and can communicate with us telepathically. They are also able to manipulate our consciousness, and augment our perceptions as such. The very large entities of up to 700cm are mostly found in mountains and valleys.[24]

Rosalind A. McKnight describes that according to the alien intelligent entities she has encountered during binaural-beat OBE sessions that trees act as a battery for humans on earth, several minutes a day underneath a tree or touching it, revitalizes us. Apparently fairies and gnomes are part of plants, wood and trees' consciousness.[25]

Graham Hancock analyses the numerous recounts of people who have observed a fairy-dance, whereby fairies hold hands in a sort of circular dance. From the many witness counts it seems that at one point during this dance, the fairies disappear. When interrupted during the dance, they could be quite violent towards the human observer.[26] He writes: "What I propose instead is that its vigorous, brisk, energetic movement and generally circular pattern may be some kind of technique - or technology, just as the San trance dance is a technology – to transmit dancers from this world to the otherworld, and back again as well."[27]

The fairy circle thus acted as some kind or portal. According to Hancock, scientific research has pointed out that the distinctive bright green patterns of fairy rings "is the result of soil enrichment due to subsurface fungal growth." He also writes that springs, wells and caves were widely believed to serve as portals. According to Hancock, Aldeus Huxley and Albert Hoffmann seem also of the impression that other realities exist, vibrating at their own specific frequencies that become visible to us in AESC.[28]

UFO Abductions
Scientific research conducted on UFO abductees has provided no evidence of mental illness in these persons.[29] This compares with findings by psychiatrist Dr. John Mack (Harvard University) who offered therapy to UFO abductees, and with those of psychologist Elizabeth Slater who tested UFO abductees. Hancock writes that both Mack and Slater concluded that the abductions may have indeed occurred, that they are real and may have manifested in this world. Hancock further writes that there are too many similarities between the realities and entities encountered by UFO abductees and shamanic trance experiences to be ignored (levitation and floating; caverns or under water worlds; therianthropes and

hybrids before appearing as humanoid beings with bug-eyes; operations and wounding).[30]

UFO Abductions seem to occur during the REM (Rapid Eye Movement) state of sleep, also called the dream-period or active-sleep during sleep. Like vivid dreams, UFO abductions can be clearly remembered. REM sleep happens during about one fifth or one quarter of the time during our night's sleep. Babies spend more time in REM then adults, but do not have the luxury of verbally recalling a dream. The amount of REM sleep seems to decrease with age. All mammals have REM sleep.

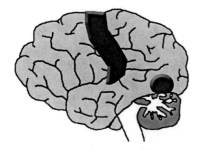 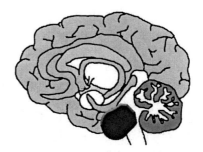

Brain areas most active during the REM state of dream-sleep (black).

Neurotransmitters norepinephrine (or noradrenaline), serotonin and histamine are little to not produced during REM sleep. Erections of the penis and clitoris are common during this period. Heart rate and breathing may increase. See also Appendix III – Neurochemicals.

Rick Strassman stated the option that there is a possibility that people who undergo UFO abductions, spontaneously overproduce DMT during that time.[31]

While during deep sleep the predominant brain wave frequency is theta or delta (between below 4-5 Hz), during REM sleep-dreaming there are peaks of 13 Hz or higher (Beta).

PART III

RECAPITULATION

TRAVELING SEQUENCING

Because of the difficult access, strict laws, scientific disproval and adherent negative media attention in our western society regarding our non-physical body, AESC, ODRs, OBEs, NDEs and UFO abductions, there is a general taboo towards exploration of one's consciousness and other dimensions of reality. In addition to this, the available methods do not guarantee a full-fledged AESC or ODR experience. Obtaining AESC through meditation and prayer, for example, may take years of practice.

However, those persons having obtained AESC and having visited ODRs have a consistency in their reporting and are absolutely certain of the objective reality of their experience (educated and non-educated persons alike). These visits often have a life-changing impact. Whereas earthly experiences may fade with time, ODR experiences seem to be vividly remembered.

Nevertheless, any legal and available method to obtaining AESC and possibly travel to an ODR requires a good preparation prior to commencement to achieve a positive result and experience:

- Being well informed about the materials and methods involved

- Preparedness and willingness to participate

- A secure and comfortable setting with possibly (a) caretaking person(s)

- Physical and mental comfort

- Either relaxation and meditative exercises (hyper quiescence → extraordinary relaxation and euphoric experience) or repetitive and rhythmic physical stimulation (hyper arousal → heightened emotional and ecstasy experience). The routing through the autonomous nervous system is different for these two methods, but the end result (euphoria or ecstasy) may give access to AESC and ODRs.

- Letting go of fear and anxiety (this being the most important factor for a positive experience). Individual fears negatively impact an AESC or ODR experience.

What the sequencing of events is prior to and during AESC and ODR visits can be different depending on the method used to obtain AESC. However, in general the following seems to occur:

- On the way to achieving AESC physical sensations such as nausea, stomach aches and nose bleeding may occur.

- Achieving AESC and visiting an ODR seems related with one's frequency and level of vibration at that moment.

- Getting into an ODR may be combined with an OBE or feeling of OBE.

- Getting into an ODR is frequently accompanied by a sound, much like breaking the sound barrier. This is also described as a crack or piercing a veil. Other descriptions are a flight through the air on a beam of light, floating and levitation.

- ODRs may obtain other (intelligent) entities and natural or non-natural surroundings. Some visits to ODRs (such as to the Hybrid or Humanoid ODR) may be subject to painful experiences in exchange for knowledge.

- When reaching the Ultimate Reality during AESC, there is a frequent observation of a tunnel and bright light, and being surrounded by beautiful voices, songs, music. Deceased friends and family may be seen and spoken with.

- When reaching the Ultimate Reality after death, there is an apparent Life Review by peers. Equally, each individual soul seems to have an interactive Life Book to learn from. Prior to returning to a physical body, the Life Review and Life Book are consulted, and a course of action and goals are outlined for the next life on earth. The body is chosen, as well as the gender, social and family environment.

- Persons obtaining an AESC or experiencing an ODR often describe the event as "more real then real", at times life changing, and describe access to it as "changing one's vibration" or "changing frequencies" or "getting to another wavelength". The higher the level of consciousness, the higher the vibration.

How AESC can be achieved through various travel methods is outlined as follows:

Travel Method	Means of AESC induction
Meditation	Stillness of the mind
Prayer	Focusing on an image
Regression Hypnosis	Obtaining very relaxed state with assistance of Hypnotherapist
Psychedelics	Inhalation or consumption of psychedelic plant(s) or fungi
Binaural beat technology	Listening through stereo headphones to binaural beat music and/or verbal guidance
Repetitive and rhythmic stimulation	Combination of rhythm (song, clapping, music, speaking in tongues) accompanied by ongoing repetitive movements (dance, flagellation, swirling)
Electric and electro-magnetic stimulation	Specialized headset through which direct stimulation of certain brain parts is achieved.
Disease	<ul><li>Brain tumors</li><li>Schizophrenia</li><li>Temporal lobe epilepsy</li></ul>
Specific locations in the world	<ul><li>Geomagnetic or electromagnetically charged locations</li></ul>

Travel Method, continued	Means of AESC induction
Water, oxygen and glucose deprivation	• Fasting on food and water • Exclusion of contact with other persons • Elimination of sound, light, smell • Self mutilation and self torture • Sleep deprivation • Hyperventilation • Shock induced (cold water)

Table 20 – Travel method and means of AESC induction

TRAVELING AND VIBRATIONAL LEVELS

Several ODRs have been described during AESC experiences (Earth, Geometric ODR, Hybrid ODR, Humanoid ODR, Earthlike ODR, Ultimate Reality, Shadow ODR). Those persons having visited ODRs describe the experience as real, and discount the notion of hallucination. Lessons learned from visits to the ODRs, and in particular to the Ultimate Reality, include a life review and insight into one's personal life book. Visits to ODRs and to earth apparently have as purpose development of the ultimate consciousness: the soul. Movement between ODRs is illustrated as going into or out of curbed spheres connected by zones that are accessed by converging vibrational rates. Transition between ODRs often is accompanied by sounds, vibrations and (bright) light. Vibrations exist in our brain in the form of brain waves, which' frequency are related to our consciousness state. Due to the frequency following response, the brain is able to resonate in conjunction with other frequencies (for example to sound as utilized in binaural beat technology). Electromagnetic charges and areas have influenced neural functions and the levels of neurochemicals, and can enhance AESC experiences (such as for example UFO abductions during REM sleep).

Non physical entities have described earth as a dense physical plane with low vibration. The physical state seems the densest of all with a very low vibrational rate. Consciousness has been explained as a level of vibration, which is altered at for example death. Since time is inversely related to the vibrational rate, time slows down when the vibrational rate increases (i.e. in the Ultimate Reality with a very high resonance, time does not exist). Emotions and stress can block vibrational energy and communication flow between different dimensions. Fear has been described as a great obstacle to human growth.

The non-physical body seems subject to gravitational forces, electricity and electro-magnetic energy. Alien entities have been witnessed at charged areas. These charged areas apparently function as portals for these entities to ODRs.

When brainwave frequencies resonate somewhere between 6.8 and 8.3 Hz consciousness and subconsciousness apparently coincide. Coincidentally, this frequency is equal to the resonant frequency of the Earth's magnetic field (also called Schumann Resonance which is on average 7.8 Hz). When brainwave frequencies resonate below 6.8 Hz and enters lower Alpha, or Theta or even Delta, a person can enter AESC and experience ODR. Deeper experiences occur during Theta and Delta. The RAS (reticular activating system) together with the thalamus plays an important role in administering brain wave frequencies in the brain. Different brainstem and limbic functions are stimulated and various neurochemicals (stress hormones, opioids, tryptamines) are released on the onset of changes in brainwave frequencies.

AESC temporarily changes the electro-chemical balance of the brain. During deep sleep (at peak hour between 02:00 hrs and 04:00 hrs) the release of the right neurochemicals (melatonin, DMT) combined with relaxation and low brainwave frequencies create the ideal circumstances for dreaming, AESC and ODR experiences (including UFO abductions). This right cocktail of brain functions, release of neurochemicals and brainwave frequencies create AESC and ODR experiences during a variety of methods, such as meditation; intense prayer; regression hypnosis; use of certain psychedelics; binaural beat technology; repetitive and rhythmic stimulation; electric or electro-magnetic stimulation of certain brain areas; disease (certain cases of schizophrenia and temporal lobe epilepsy); deprivation of water, oxygen and glucose; induction of repetitive self mutilation and pain. The same circumstances occur at certain charged locations.

At the quantum level, particles vibrate constantly. So do our neutrons, protons, electrons and so on. Their frequencies are directly related to their behavior and state. Likewise, frequencies and vibrations of our mind and body and body parts (brain) point to our states of consciousness, and access to AESC and ODR. According to information received by Rosalind A. McKnight, the basic form of communication, which is the mind, is on a wavelength that is on a very high rate of vibration on the earth level. Unfortunately, we are taught *what* to think instead of *how* to think. She has received information during her OBE travels that our mind is capable to tap into all knowledge that exists.

Brainwave frequencies and levels of vibrations are frequently mentioned by researchers of AESC and ODR, as well as by persons undergoing AESC and visiting ODR. Brainwaves are responsible for our sate of alertness (consciousness). Messages received by alien intelligent entities often refer to frequencies and levels of vibrations as a means to AESC and ODR. On asking why, the following has been responded:

- Each person's vibratory level is unique, like a fingerprint.

- Earth, for example, is considered dense, and having a low vibration energy. Our universe is on the same vibration as the particles that make up our bodies, which is why we can see it. Each galaxy is described as a cluster of atoms operating on the same vibration.

- The densest state to be in seems the physical state and being in a three-dimensional environment. Since time appears inversely related to the vibrational rate, time appears faster on earth compared to planes of high vibration (where there is no time/space).

- On earth, human thought has the highest vibration. This may be related to the "mind is pure energy" argument.

- Communication between earth and other dimensions seem to occur via or over thought waves. Other dimensions exist at another frequency.

- The purest known energy that exists is love.

- At death we change in vibration from a dense physical state to a higher vibration of the soul (the etheric self).

Other dimensions are not necessarily far away. Sylvia Browne explains that the Ultimate Reality is located in another dimension about 3 feet (1 meter) above our ground. Michael Newton refers to going to other dimensions as traveling via zones that are opened and closed by converging vibrational attunement. Robert A. Monroe described how his vibration energy changes during relaxation to about 27-60Hz and onward to reach an OBE state at about 10-18Hz. Consciousness seems related to vibration levels, as apparently we keep reincarnating until our desired level of vibration (consciousness) is reached. The subconsciousness seems the storage area of all past and future lives, including experiences obtained during our "in between-lives" at the Ultimate Reality. The largest obstacle to growth and obtaining AESC is fear. Fear-based human creations such as "hell", and violence described during ODR experiences are explained as the expression of our own negative (low vibrating) emotions.

Graham Hancock quotes a patient of psychiatrist John Mack (known for counseling UFO abductees) as saying: "..they have to alter your vibration in order to get a solid object to pass through another solid object, literally."[1]

Rick Strassman writes that it is possible that DMT alters the characteristics of our brains, allowing us to perceive other realities.[2] His subjects stated: "There was the same pulsating vibration. They wanted me to join them, to stay with them. I was tempted."[3] "I watched the universe's creation down from fundamental mental energy to a vibratory rate to material things."[4] "..vast energy slowing to vibrations, finally resulting in matter."[5]

Strassman also indicates that many UFO abductees describe high-frequency vibrations at the onset of their voyage, making them feel as if they come apart at the molecular level. He has a theory about DMT being the transmission or receiver trigger to AESC and ODRs: "DMT provides regular, repeated, and reliable access to "other" channels. The other planes of existence are always there. In fact they are right here, transmitting all the time! But we cannot perceive them because we are not designed to do so; our hard-wiring keeps us tuned in to Channel Normal. It takes only a second or two – a few heartbeats the spirit molecule requires to make its way to the brain – to change the channel, to open our minds to these other planes or existence."[6] "Perhaps just the right amount of DMT is involved in the brain's maintenance of the correct receiving properties. That is, it keeps our brains tuned in to Channel Normal."[7]

Albert Hoffmann, the Swiss scientist who first synthesized LSD also suggests that the brain may act as a receiver once biochemically altered. As quoted by Graham Hancock, Hoffmann wrote: "Since the endless variety and diversity of the universe correspond to infinitely many different wavelengths, depending on the adjustment of the receiver, many different realities can become conscious. The true importance of LSD and related hallucinogenics lies in their capacity to shift the wavelength setting of the receiving "self", and thereby evoke alternations in reality consciousness."[8]

Rhawn Joseph argues that the same occurs:"...when fasting, isolated, in pain, under LSD, in trance, or in the throes of religious ecstasy, all of which activates the limbic system thus increasing channel capacity, so that what is concealed is revealed."[9] "Hallucinogens are said to enable an individual to peer between the space that separate this reality from all other realities, such that what is concealed is suddenly revealed. It is the amygdale, hippocampus, and temporal lobe which are responsible for these complex hallucinations, and it is the amygdale which normally filters much of this information so that it remains hidden. Hence, by hyper activating these structures, in essence, on is also activating the *transmitter* to God."[10]

TRAVELING AND NEURAL FUNCTIONS

The brain is divided horizontally (into hemispheres), vertically (brainstem to cerebellum), and functionally (different lobes). It seems that each state of consciousness is interfaced with a different part of the brain. Different methods of AESC induction activate different parts of the brain, however all methods kick start specific brain functions, in particular in the brainstem (mainly the raphe nuclei, locus coeruleus, RAS) and in the limbic structures (mainly the amygdala, thalamus, hypothalamus, hippocampus), and release certain neurochemicals with as combined result low brainwave frequencies and limbic activation.

There are a specific set of neural functions that take place during AESC. According to Rhawn Joseph: "..limbic structures such as the amygdale, hippocampus, and inferior temporal lobe have been repeatedly shown to subserve and provide the foundations for mystical, spiritual, religious experience, and the perception, including the "hallucination" of ghosts, demons, spirits and sprites, and belief in demonic or angelic possession."[1]

Stimulation of the limbic structures temporal lobe, amygdala, hippocami can lead to pleasant or fearful experiences, depending if the person is able to relax and let go of the fear-response. While both brain functions operate at both sides of the brain, and various neurotransmitters are being released, there seems to be a difference in hemispheric activity during pleasant and unpleasant AESC.

When negative emotions lead during the experience and own personal fears are being expressed, there is a predominant activation at <u>right hemispheric</u> brain functions (integrative, holistic, our core self untouched by the human body). This can be the case, for example, with persons using psychedelics, undergoing repetitive physical stimulation, or those suffering from temporal lobe epilepsy or schizophrenia. The right hemisphere (and thus right amygdale and right hippocampus) is more involved compared to the left hemisphere in the production of religious imagery and related emotions. The right hemisphere is also highly active during REM state (rapid eye movement whereby the brain seems quite active and body musculature is paralyzed, during deep sleep and dreaming), while during this state the left hemisphere is less active. Persinger showed that (right) temporal lobe activation can provide a "God" experience or occurrence of a presence. Olaf Blanke has shown that right angular gyrus stimulation can result in OBEs.

Left hemispheric brain functions (analytical, rational, our core self modified by the human body) seem to be more active during for example meditation and prayer, which usually lead to pleasant experiences. On the contrary, the left hemisphere shows a strongly diminished activity during deep hypnosis. The left hemisphere shows more *variation* in brainwave activity during spontaneous obtained OBE by Robert A. Monroe, while his brain wave frequencies were similar in both hemispheres. Coincidentally, the left thalamus of practicing Tibetan monks and Franciscan nuns is more active during rest than the right thalamus, which is unusual.

Brainwave frequencies seem governed by certain brain areas (raphe nuclei, locus coeruleus, reticular activating system RAS, thalamus) who release certain neurochemicals such as acetylcholine, norepinephrine (or noradrenaline) and serotonin). These chemicals in turn inhibit or excite other brain areas, causing symptoms of relaxation or stress. According to Rhawn Joseph, mediated by the brain stem nuclei, the amygdale may trigger the first phase of dreaming (REM) when the hippocampus begins to produce slow wave, theta activity.[2]

The similarities between different AESC as induced by different methods are evident. Rhawn Joseph concludes that:

"..dreaming, trance states, depth electrode activation, extreme fear, traumatic injury, or temporal lobe epilepsy, result in hyperactivation of the amygdale and hippocampus and overlying temporal lobe. These structures create an image of the individual floating or even soaring above familiar or bizarre surroundings, and will trigger memories, hallucinations, brilliant lights, as well as secrete opiate-like neurochemicals which induce a state of euphoria and thus eternal peace and harmony."[3]

Kelly Bulkeley writes: "The close relationship in many cultures between dreams, visions, trances, artistic inspiration, and other extraordinary modes of consciousness suggests that at least some features of dream formation do not depend on REM sleep but can be activated in a variety of other mind/brain conditions."[4]

Michael A. Persinger states: "If the temporal lobe had developed in some other way, the God experience would not have occurred. I am not contending that the God experience is localized within the temporal lobe, nor more than vision is stored within the occipital lobe or the body image is stored within the parietal region. Instead, my hypothesis is that the God experience is a phenomenon that is associated with the construction of the temporal lobe."[5]

Everybody with a functioning brain (psychotic or non-psychotic) seems to be able to obtain AESC and to visit ODRs. Within the brain, predominantly the right hemispheric limbic system, brainstem and low brainwave frequencies (vibrations originating from the brainstem and limbic system) are active participants to obtain a spiritual and OBE experiences, achieve AESC and to visit ODRs.

- Low brainwave frequencies of Theta or Delta are essential to achieve access to the subconscious mind and to allow for AESC and/or OBE to occur. They also seem essential to ODR with another (often higher) vibration then earth. Repetition and rhythm may bring the brain into a resonating frequency. High brainwave frequencies transpire during fear, anxiety and stress, and interfere negatively with the AESC and ODR experience.

• Brain wave patterns are governed by the raphe nuclei, locus coeruleus, RAS (reticular activating system) together with the thalamus. The hippocampus balances the fear response of the amygdala (which contains the seat of fear and anxiety) and is also a producer of Theta activity during REM sleep. The hypothalamus and thalamus together initiate levels of alertness (consciousness). The brainstem and thalamus increase in activity during AESC. An increased thalamus activity makes a (spiritual) experience feel real. Stress hormones NE (norepinephrine or noradrenaline) and cortisol levels are generally low during relaxed states of AESC, but as exception may spike during psychedelic use most likely as a result of personal fears. The locus coeruleus is responsible for the physiological response to stress and panic, when it releases NE. Cortisol levels are low during relaxation and are released during stress and anxiety. Cortisol is produced by the adrenal cortex in the brain, under control of the pituitary gland and hypothalamus.

• The primary and primitive structures of the limbic system (temporal lobe, thalamus, hypothalamus, amygdala, hippocampus) produce hallucinations, OBE sensations and other feelings similar to AESC experiences, such as spiritual or mystic experiences. The frontal lobes and several neurochemicals (such as serotonin) filter these sensations before they reach the amygdala. Scans have pointed out that the amygdala, thalamus and hippocampus are active during AESC. Strong fluctuations of opioids, tryptamines and stress hormones impact the amygdala and hippocampus. At the onset of AESC, the temporal lobe is stimulated, which onward stimulates the amygdala and hippocampus, which in turn may create a supernatural experience.

- The pineal gland is active during low brain wave states and in darkness. It produces the tryptamines melatonin and DMT out of serotonin.

- The tryptamine serotonin is produced by the neurons of the raphe nuclei and is replaced by psychedelics with a tryptamine's core (LSD, iboga, psilocybin) or by another tryptamine (DMT). During non-psychedelic induced AESC serotonin and melatonin levels rise. Tryptamine melatonin is at its peak during REM sleep and during relaxation/visualization when brainwave frequencies are between Theta and Delta.

- The frequency following response allows for the brain to resonate to a binaural beat, and thus instigate a brainwave state. Rick Strassman opted the idea that tryptamine DMT may be produced during REM sleep at Theta and Delta, as the pineal gland may resonate at this frequency, thus releasing DMT. This may explain why during NDE, OBE and UFO abductions DMT levels are high. In the event of great stress, fear or panic excess NE (norepinephrine or noradrenaline) and epinephrine (adrenaline) may also stimulate DMT production, resulting in a negative AESC experience.

- Opiods (or endorphins, such as beta-endorphin and encephalin) are released by the neurons of the hypothalamus and by the pituitary gland. Opioids reduce fear and pain, while at the same time soliciting a euphoric response. They are released during both strenuous and relaxation activities.

- A change in brainwave state (which is an electromagnetic state) follows with an alteration of the electrochemical environment of the brain, which in turn enhances or reduces a person's altered state.

- During AESC, blood flow increase to the (left) frontal lobes changes the orientation of the self in a space, while decrease of blood flow to the parietal lobes manipulates spatial orientation and 3D body imaging.

- The right hemisphere (our original energy untouched by the human body: holistic) seems more responsible for unpleasant experiences, visions of The Divine, NDEs and OBEs.

HIPPOCAMPI

The hippocampus does not directly generate emotion (unlike the amygdale and hypothalamus), but exerts great influence on an individual's state of mind. Records experiences and arranges storage in long term memory (such as during meditation, prayer and psychedelics use). And it balances the fear response of the amygdale. Rats, during a self-stimulation experience of their hippocampi, preferred it over food and sex.

Activity may become weakened during fear, when stress hormones are released. It thus balances the fear-response of the amygdale, with which it plays an interdependent role in regard to memory. Producer of slow wave, theta activity during REM.
Is stimulated by for example rhythm and dance. When stimulated may create a visual hallucination of the body and surroundings and OBE. When damaged, will not be able to construct *new* memory.

Once the hippocampus is inactivated or damaged, it is difficult to form new memories, while old memories may remain (such as might happen due to oxygen deprivation, epilepsy or Alzheimer's).

Activation Right Hippocampus

Gives memory and dreamlike hallucinations.

TEMPORAL LOBE & AMYGDALA

Together process dreams and (emotional) memories.
If both the right   mygdale and temporal lobes are removed, dreams no longer occur and hallucinations are reduced.

Stimulation of both temporal lobes and   mygdale simultaneous provides sexual, religious, or spiritual experiences and (frightening) hallucinations.

Symbols, such as crosses, circles and triangles can activate the temporal lobe and amygdale. Rhythm sequencing (sound, dance, chant, song) stimulates the temporal lobe which in turn activates the   mygdale and hippocampus, which can result in supernatural experiences.

HIPPOCAMPI & AMYGDALA
Activation of both the amygdale and hippocampus can result in bizarre, sexual and fearful imagery; as well as visions of demons, ghosts, God and entities; and hallucinations outside the cognitive map such as OBE.

AMYGDALA
Control center for the display, storage and experience of emotions and moods. Responsible for dreams and emotional memories Once activated (resulting in fear and anxiety) it activates in turn the hypothalamus and hippocampus.

Once the amygdala is removed, a person cannot interpret negative emotions.

May become overactive during fear, when stress hormones and endogenous opioids are released.

When serotonin release is blocked (such as with use of psychedelics), the amygdale increases activity.

An overactive amygdala may cause fear and anxiety, and processes information that is normally suppressed.

The amygdala contain opiate producing and receiving neurons. High concentrates of opiates create calm and euphoria.

Activation Left Amygdala	Activation Right Amygdala
Overall pleasant experience and a presence may be felt on the right side of the body.

When the left amygdala is destroyed, dreaming continues. | In general the experience is unpleasant and a presence may be felt on the left side of the body

When the right amygdala is destroyed, dreaming stops. Visual hallucinations, body sensations, déjà vu's, illusions, gustatory or alimentary experiences (stomach aches) such may happen during repetitive physical stimulation and use of psychedelics |

TEMPORAL LOBE

Chronic hyper stimulation of the temporal lobes, such as during seizures results in feeling more sensed presences.

Electrical activity in the temporal lobe is related to the different brain wave states (beta, alpha, theta, delta).

Activation Left Temporal Lobe	Activation Right Temporal Lobe
Presence felt on right side of body combined with a general pleasant spiritual experience. If the left temporal lobe is not functioning, dreaming is still possible.	Presence felt on left side of body, and the experience may be fearful (with possible ghosts, demons, devils, or messages from The Divine depending on the person's belief system).

THALAMI & HYPOTHALAMI

The thalamus transmits sensory impulses, except smell, to the cerebral cortex. Together with the hypothalamus it initiates sleep and levels of alertness (states of consciousness).

Receives signals from RAS and then negotiates what state to be in, particularly when it comes to Alpha and Beta. Responsible for transition to Delta and higher states. Brainwave patterns are governed by the thalamus, RAS, locus oeruleus and raphe nuclei. Makes experiences feel real and lucid during meditation, prayer and spiritual regression hypnosis. The ypothalamus, like the amygdala, contains opiate producing and receiving neurons.

Activation Left Thalamus

Is more active *during rest* by practicing meditating monks and praying nuns. This is unusual.

PREFRONTAL CORTEX Part of frontal lobe

A region of the frontal lobe involved in cognitive behavior and motor planning. Provides intense and maintained concentration and attention during meditation, prayer and spiritual regression hypnosis.

Activation Left Prefrontal Cortex	Activation Right Prefrontal Cortex
Activates more while listening to joyful, happy music. Cognitive processing and behavior during spiritual regression hypnosis.	Activates more while listening to fearful, sad music.

PARIETALLOBE: Left Hemisphere activation
Involved in processing language, spatial orientation, and semantic representation
Reduction in activity, results in reduction in sense of space and time, fading of self into non self and obtaining a sense of unity among objects and self during meditation and prayer.
If hyper stimulated, provides a feeling of a presence behind the body.
Left angular gyrus activation (part of inferior parietal lobe) provides feeling of presence behind the body. *Right angular gyrus* activation provides OBE.
Anterior cingulated giri respond to errors and evaluates outcomes during spiritual regression hypnosis.

RAS & ERTAS
Reticular activating system and Extended reticular thalamic activating system. Both located in the brain stem
In order to alter consciousness it is necessary to provide some sort of information input to the RAS. RAS (being part of ERTAS) interprets and reacts to *information* from internal and external stimuli by regulating arousal states, attention-focus and the level of awareness; critical elements of consciousness itself.
RAS instigates changes in brainwave activity. It transmits facilitator signals to the thalamus, which in turn excites the cortex, which in return excites the thalamus, thus creating a reverberating circuit that makes make one wake up in the morning. RAS, thalamus, locus coeruleus and raphe nuclei together govern brainwave patterns.
RAS is also activated during binaural beat stimulation. However, it reduces in activity during spiritual regression hypnosis.

PINEAL GLAND
The small endocrine pineal gland is active during deeper states of consciousness, when brain wave frequencies are lowest, such as during deep sleep and meditation. The pineal gland is active in darkness, and little active by light.
Source of DMT production. Pineal gland (first DMT production) is first visible at a fetus of 49 days, when DMT is first produced. At this time the male/female gender is designated. 49 Days is described in the Tibetan book of the Dead as the time in which a soul reincarnates. DMT is flooding the body at death, which could explain NDE. During intense emotions there is more DMT production. Produces melatonin out of serotonin.

Table 21 - Brain Function, Activity and Related Feelings during different methods of obtaining AESC, and during activation of either the left or right hemisphere.

Neurochemicals: Tryptamines	
Seratonin	
Found in all plant and animal life Restricts perceptual and information processing, contracts muscle lining of veins and arteries. Neurons of raphe nuclei in the brainstem are the principal source of serotonin release in the brain.	**Increase** Increases a little during meditation, prayer and related practices. When serotonin levels are too high, anxiety, insomnia and sexual dysfunction are its symptoms. No increase during use of certain psychedelics, as the body allows serotonin to be replaced in its receptor sites by DMT or Psilocybin (who both contain tryptamine) and by Iboga or LSD (who both contain a tryptamine core). **Decrease** During dream states. When serotonin production is too low, panic and depression sets in.
Malatonin	
Found in all plant and animal life Depresses the central nervous system and reduces pain sensitivity. Noradrenaline and adrenaline stimulate melatonin production during great stress and fear. In the pineal gland melatonin is created out of selatonin (serotonin is first acetylated and then methylated)	**Increase** Highest during sleep between 02:00 hrs and 04:00 hrs, when also most temporal lobe seizures and UFO abductions occur. During this time REM sleep is activated and the brain wave frequencies vibrate in the Theta and Delta state. During this time also more UFO abductions, augmentation in temporal lobe seizure activity. During relaxation, visualization and related practices melatonin production is high as well. No increase during certain psychedelics use (see above). **Decrease** When geomagnetic activity above 20nT. Low melatonin production enhances sexual functions. Suppression when geomagnetic activity is above 40nT, certain temporal lobe seizures may increase

Neurochemicals: Tryptamines, continued	
DMT	
In the pineal gland, seratonin undergoes "methyltransferase" (attachment of a CH_3 methylgroup) twice so methylate-tryptamine becomes DMT (di-methyl-tryptamine). The body has a priority of psychedelics containing DMT above others, since DMT is also naturally made by the body itself.	**Increase** Possible that during induced great stress and fear (including sexual activity, orgasm, psychosis) adrenaline and noradrenaline are released, which in turn stimulate melatonin production (see above) which in turn stimulates DMT production. Stress can worsen delusions and hallucinations in psychotic patients. It is possible that during theta deep sleep, meditation, binaural beat technology and related practices surrounding brain tissue resonates in low vibration, including the pineal gland, resulting in DMT production. This may explain NDE, OBE and UFO abductions during REM sleep

Neurochemicals: Stress Hormones	
NE	
Norepinephrine = noradrenaline Increases alertness. Released from released from noradrenergic neurons of the locus coeruleus in the brain.	**Increase** During fear, which can be due to psychedelics or disease. **Decrease** During meditation, prayer and related practices.
Cortisol	
Produced by adrenal cortex in the brain is under control of the pituitary gland and hypothalamus. Highest levels found during early morning when we wake up. Cortisol increases blood pressure and blood sugar levels, and decreases the immune system.	**Increase** During fear, which can be due to psychedelics or disease. **Decrease** During meditation, prayer and related practices.

Neurochemicals: Endorphins (endogenous opioids)	
Beta-endorphin	
Depresses respiration, reduces fear and pain, produces sensations of joy and euphoria. It is found in neurons of the hypothalamus, as well as the pituitary gland. Changes in rhythm, not in levels during meditation, prayer and related practices.	**Increases** During psychedelics use and with repetitive physical stimulation combined with physical exertion, such as during exhaustive physical dance and clapping; extreme temperature differences in cold or sweat lodges; water and food deprivation; flagellation.
Encephalin	
Acts as pain blocker. It is found in neurons of the hypothalamus, as well as the pituitary gland.	**Increase** During use of psychedelics and with repetitive physical stimulation combined with physical exertion, such as during exhaustive physical dance and clapping; extreme temperature differences in cold or sweat lodges; water and food deprivation; flagellation.

Table 22 – Neurochemical activity during different methods of obtaining AESC and other states of mind.

TRAVELING AND CURRENT LAWS

All religions seem to have a shamanic origin, whereby a person (the messenger) receives information during AESC (often accompanied by a visit to ODR). This direct and personal experience has often been depicted in cave art. Henceforth through the ages the various personal AESC and ODR experiences have been translated by established religious organizations into books, rules and regulations together with rituals and traditions. Over time, the original and personal shamanic experience became further and further removed from the source. The original messenger has often become a Messiah or Saint, and the interpretation of the message is woven into the fabric of the religion who adopted it. The original message is now explained by intermediaries (clerics) to the masses. Almost all (monotheistic) religions prohibit the intermediaries and the masses to undergo AESC, with few exceptions such as the Pentecostal church where speaking in tongues is encouraged (but no ODRs seem reached). Current shamanic-based (polytheistic) religions still accept practices to obtain AESC.

Psychedelics are outlawed in most countries, so psychedelic-induced AESC exploration is difficult (even in a private setting). Society and religion over time have restricted exploration of our own consciousness, and have restricted certain plant and fungi consumption. Scientific research is nearly non-existence when it comes to psychedelics-induced AESC or to any other induced AESC for that matter. Current research in a laboratory-type setting into AESC and ODRs is done through means of binaural beat technology (Monroe Institute) or through direct electric and electro-magnetic stimulation of certain brain areas (Persinger).

This leaves only certain legal and non-laboratory-type

methods available to the general public, such as meditation, prayer and spiritual regression hypnosis. Binaural beat technology CDs are available for purchase at various websites. Induction of AESC through means of repetition and rhythm (music, dance, drumming, clapping, swirling, etc.) occur at most shamanic based religions. A popularized derivative of these exists for the general public, such as through organized gatherings and specialized retreats. Water, oxygen and glucose deprivation techniques are also frequently induced at these alternatives for the interesting participants (sweat lodges, cold lodges, fasting, hyperventilation, breathing techniques, strenuous physical activities, etc.).

NEUROTHEOLOGY AND FUTURE RESEARCH

There seems a (biological) basis in the brain for spiritual experience, for altered and expanded states of consciousness, and for other dimensions of reality. The brain is the essential trigger and a requirement to achieving these experiences, states and realities. These experiences, states and realities occur only when specific and certain brain functions, brainwaves and neurochemicals operate together with certain AESC/ODR means and methods. There are various (legal and illegal) means and methods to obtaining these experiences, states and realities.

Rick Strassman: "..the regularity and consistency of these reports [of subjects' ODR experience during DMT], and the strength of the sense of reality behind them, supported a biological explanation. We were activating certain hard-wired sites in the brain that elicit a display of visions and feelings in the mind. How else could so many people report similar experiences: insect-like, reptilian creatures?"[1]

Even if it is agreed that AESC and ODR experiences *originate* in the brain, and that various brain functions and release of various neurotransmitters are required in order to obtain these experiences, there are two schools of thought related to whether these experiences *remain* in the brain or not. One of the schools of thought claims that it's *all in the brain* because of our brain's design. Their argument is that depersonalization (when a person feels detached from his/her body) is a result of mixing the self (frontal lobe based) with emotions (temporal lobe based), since both increase in activation during AESC. Imaging, dreamlike states and ODR are argued to be a result of memory release of one's life experience. No distinction is seen between a psychotic and a non-psychotic experience, other then that the latter is more controlled.

The other school of thought (as supported by this book) claims that AESC and ODR experiences occur *in the brain and beyond*. Their argument is that our consciousness is not part of our ego or self, is not solely brain-based, and can travel beyond the realm of the body to explore AESC and ODR. The researchers of this school of thought validate the possibility of other (non-physical) dimensions beyond our earth-based (physical) dimension. The brain in this school of thought is seen as a portal to other dimensions. The experiences of reaching AESC and ODRs has changed the life and death perspective of participants, who describe the experience as more real then real.

They make a clear distinction between a psychotic and a non-psychotic experience, whereby the latter is experienced as real and uplifting, and involves a loss of pride and ego. This compared to psychotic hallucinations, which are often experienced as unplanned and often unwanted, confusing, not real, often negative, and include feelings of self-importance.

However real and profound the spiritual experiences, altered states, and other dimensions of realities are, there is to date no scientific process found to validate their existence. This does not imply that they do not exist, but indicates that these cannot be (sufficiently) measured according to the current scientific method.

Andrew Newberg, Eugene d'Aguili and Vince Rause suggest that: "..scientific research supports the possibility that a mind can exist without ego, that awareness can exist without self."[2] "..our research has left us no choice but to conclude that the mystics may be on to something, that the mind's machinery of transcendence may in fact be a window through which we can glimpse the ultimate realness of something that is truly divine."[3]

Graham Hancock writes: "It is very difficult to understand how the human mind without any real, objective and consistent external stimulus, could consistently generate the same bizarre sequence of unexpected procedures and experiences in two groups of people as far apart culturally as shamans in hunter-gatherer societies and UFO abductees in the United States."[4] "People all over the world have massively recurrent shared cross-cultural experiences in situations where science can see no evidence for any external world."[5]

Graham Hancock writes of his own AESC experiences with psychedelics :
"Of beings that are absolutely real in some modality not yet understood by science, that exist around us and with us, that even seem to be aware of us and to take an active interest in us, but that vibrate at a frequency beyond the range of our senses and instruments and thus generally remain completely visible to us."[6]

Several important questions remain, and require future in depth neurotheological research:

- the (biological) purpose of obtaining AESC

- the vibrations related to AESC and ODRs

- the lessons to be learned from ODRs

- whether AESC and ODRs exist only in, or only outside, or in & outside of our brain

Terence McKenna questions why tryptamines are the least explored psychedelic by science, while they are the most common hallucinogens in organic nature. McKenna suggests that: "..intelligent, thoughtful people should take psychedelics and try and understand what's going on. Not groups of prisoners, not graduate students, but mature, intelligent people need to share their experiences."[7]

Meta analysis of AESC and ODR research could, on basis of occurrences, similarities and descriptions, provide insight of these phenomena related to neurotheology. Meta analysis joins the results of various studies that address a similar set of related research hypotheses and theories. This method allows for quantification and qualification from various sources in a scientifically accepted manner.

Current day scanning and brain-imaging techniques should be able to identify areas in the brain which are activated during AESC and ODR visits during the many types of induction (meditation, hypnosis, binaural beat technology, repetitive & rhythmic stimulation, psychedelic use, etc.). Since the brain can create images that don't exist on earth, research should extend into how this is possible. At the same time, neurochemical levels and brain wave frequencies should be monitored.

The "expedition" results of participants should be analyzed and mapped. Alien intelligent entities and life forms could be identified according to the Linnaean taxonomy for classification of living species. Specific alien cultures should be identified and recognized according to anthropological standards. Educative information obtained in ODRs should be documented and compared. If AESC and ODR were treated as if exploring new lands, other planets and galaxies, and if alien (intelligent) entities were treated as newly discovered species, the common consensus of taboo surrounding neurotheology would be eased, and research its subject matter would be (scientifically) accepted.

PART IV

APPENDICES

BRAIN STEM

Brainstem: Olivary Nucleus and Inferior Colliculus

The brainstem's superior olivary nucleus in each hemisphere is the area in the brain where auditory input is first integrated and transmitted via neurons. It then goes to the "reticular activating system" or RAS (part of ERTAS, as described in next subchapter), where it can instigate changes in brainwave activity. The reticular activating system (RAS)

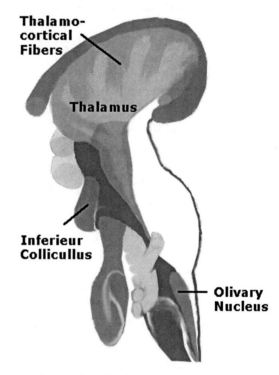

transmits facilitator signals to the thalamus (see Appendix II – Limbic System). The thalamus excites the cortex, and the cortex then excites the thalamus in a reverberating circuit. Such a positive feedback loop is what wakes us up in the morning. During the day external stimuli and internal factors, including inhibitory interneurons, balance the different activity levels.[1]

Impaired consciousness is caused by malfunction of the

neurons in the RAS, and the impairment has at least three levels. Sopor or clouding of consciousness is a term for reduced wakefulness, stupor is a sleepy state from which the patient can be aroused by vigorous stimuli, and coma is an unresponsive state of unconsciousness from which the patient cannot be awakened even with the most vigorous stimuli.[2]

In the case of binaural beat stimulation, the frequency following response apparently originates from the inferior colliculus located underneath the thalamus.[3]

The tryptamine serotonin is produced by the neurons of the brain stem's raphe nuclei.

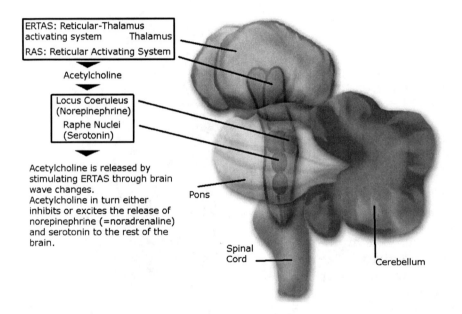

ERTAS: Reticular-Thalamus activating system   Thalamus

RAS: Reticular Activating System

Acetylcholine

Locus Coeruleus (Norepinephrine)
Raphe Nuclei (Serotonin)

Acetylcholine is released by stimulating ERTAS through brain wave changes.
Acetylcholine in turn either inhibits or excites the release of norepinephrine (=noradrenaline) and serotonin to the rest of the brain.

Pons

Spinal Cord

Cerebellum

Brainstem: ERTAS and RAS

ERTAS means extended reticular thalamic activating system i.e. the brainstem reticular formation or intralaminar nuclei of the thalamus. According to D. Brian Brady: "The word reticular means 'net-like' and the neural reticular formation itself is a large, net-like diffuse area of the brainstem. Further he explains, relating to various research: "The RAS regulates cortical EEG and controls arousal, attention, and awareness - the elements of consciousness itself."[4]

ERTAS may be the neural mechanism behind observable brainwave changes according to F. Holmes Atwater.[4] He also states that brainwave patterns are governed by certain brain areas (thalamus, reticular activating system RAS, locus coeruleus, raphe nuclei), who release certain chemicals (acetylcholine, norepinephrine or noradrenaline and serotonin – see also Appendix III - Neurochemicals). These chemicals in turn inhibit or excite other brain areas, causing symptoms of relaxation or stress.

Atwater quotes from research performed by Empson: "RAS (being part of ERTAS) interprets and reacts to *information* from internal and external stimuli by regulating arousal states, attention-focus and the level of awareness; critical elements of consciousness itself."[5] "How we interpret, respond and react to information then, is managed by ERTAS stimulating the thalamus and cortex."[6]

Atwater continues stating that within the ERTAS model, changes in socio-psychological conditioning not only directly alter the content of consciousness (i.e. new thoughts, unique ideas, novel concepts), but also alter the arousal level associated with such content.

Limbic System: Amygdala

The amygdale is an almond-shaped neural structure located in the anterior part of the temporal lobe of the cerebrum; intimately connected with the hypothalamus, hippocampus and the cingulate gyrus; as part of the limbic system it plays an important role in motivation and emotional behavior. It is the control center for the display and experience of emotions and moods.[1]

Andrew Newberg and Mark Robert Waldman write that epileptics who have had their amygdale removed have difficulty to respond with negative emotions.[2] On the contrary, they write: "...a person with an overactive amygdale will often live in a constant state of fear or anxiety."[3]

The amygdala is also described as a small structure lying in the medial temporal lobe which is important for the emotional content of new memories (remembering and evaluation).[4] It is also called amygdaloid nucleus. Carol Raush Albright and James B. Ashbrook describe the amygdale as the gatekeeper of "selective attention" between our senses and emotions.[5]

Andrew Newberg, Eugene d'Aguili and Vince Rause write that the amygdale increases its activity during arousal states, which in turn activates the hypothalamus, which in turn influences the activity of the autonomic nervous system. Likewise the hippocampus is greatly influenced by the activity of the amygdale.[6]

Rhawn Joseph outlines that the amygdale enables an individual to re-experience memories and emotions such as love, mystical experiences, ecstasy associated with orgasm, and the dread of terror. He also writes that the amygdale is capable of processing visual, tactile, auditory, gustatory, and emotional stimuli simultaneously. The frontal lobes and a variety of neurochemicals including serotonin (5HT) filter these senses before they reach the amygdale. Joseph continues in the same chapter with stating that abnormal activation of the amygdale and temporal lobe can also induce frightening hallucinations, since fear is the most common reaction associated with amygdale activation.[7] He also maintains that: "Similar explanations could be offered in regard to the spiritual significance attributed to triangles, circles, hands, and eyes. The amygdale and overlaying temporal lobe also become activated in response to these perceptual stimuli. In fact, crosses, triangles and circles were etched on the Cro-Magnon cave walls over 35,000 years ago, whereas hands and eyes repeatedly appear in mystical contexts."[8] As example he states that when staring at a cross, the temporal lobes and the amygdale become activated.

Rhawn Joseph points out that the amygdale, its overlaying temporal lobe and associated limbic system, are the neurological seat for dreams and (emotional) memories.[9] He further quotes excerpts from various researchers: "The amygdale, in conjunction with the hippocampus, contributes in large part to the production of very sexual as well as bizarre, unusual and fearful mental phenomenon including out-of-body disassociate states, feelings of depersonalization, and hallucinogenic and dreamlike recollections involving threatening men, naked women, sexual intercourse, religion, the experience of God, as well as demons and ghosts and pigs walking upright dressed as people." [10]

Limbic System: Hippocampus

The hippocampus is a complex neural structure (shaped like a sea horse) consisting of gray matter and located on the floor of each lateral ventricle; intimately involved in motivation and emotion as part of the limbic system; has a central role in the formation of memories.[11] The hippocampus serves both to consolidate *and* to construct memory.[12] It is an ancient part of the mammalian brain evolved directly from the olfactory bulb, which explains why emotions are easily aroused by familiar which explains why emotions are easily aroused by familiar scents.[13]

Andrew Newberg and Mark Robert Waldman write that the hippocampus helps to balance the fear-response of the amygdale. They also emphasize that strong emotions can radically change our perceptions of reality.[14] The hippocampus is also described as a brain structure which lies under the medial temporal lobe, one on each side of the brain.[15] It is further described as follows: "It is sometimes grouped with other nearby structures including the dentate gyrus and called the "hippocampal formation.""[16]

The hippocampus is critical for the formation of new autobiographical and fact memories. It may function as a memory "gateway" through which new memories must pass before entering permanent storage in the brain. It is the gateway to the experience of images. The hippocampus is involved in learning and long lasting long-term memory. This is what makes hippocampus the decision-maker.[17]

The hippocampus and amygdale play an interdependent role in regard to memory according to Rhawn Joseph. According to Joseph it appears that the amygdale is responsible for storing the emotional aspects, personal reactions to events and emotional memory formation and recall; whereas the hippocampus acts to store and recall of the cognitive, visual, verbal, spatial and contextual details in memory.[18]

Andrew Newberg, Eugene d'Aguili and Vince Rause describe that amygdale activity influences the hippocampus.[19] They also write that: "Unlike the amygdale and the hypothalamus, the hippocampus does not directly generate emotion, but by its regulatory effects upon other key parts of the brain, it exerts great influence upon an individual's state of mind."[20]

Catherine E. Meyers states: "Hippocampal damage can result in anterograde amnesia: loss of ability to form new memories, although older memories may be safe. Thus, someone who sustains an injury to the hippocampus may have good memory of his childhood and the years before the injury, but relatively little memory for anything that happened since. Some memories, such as the memory for new skills or habits, can sometimes be formed even without the hippocampus. A current research area is to determine exactly what kinds of learning and memory can survive hippocampal damage, and how these kinds of learning can be used to guide rehabilitation. The hippocampus is especially sensitive to global reductions in oxygen level in the body. Thus, periods of oxygen deprivation (hypoxia) which are not fatal may nonetheless result in particular damage to the hippocampus. This could occur during a heart attack, respiratory failure, sleep apnea, carbon monoxide poisoning, near-drowning, etc. The hippocampus is also a common focus site in epilepsy, and can be damaged through chronic seizures. It is also sometimes damaged in diseases such as herpes encephalitis, and is one of the first brain areas to show damage in Alzheimer's disease."[21]

Scott Atran writes that the hippocampus helps to link the intentions behind verbal and vocal signals to suitable arousal and emotional states via the amygdale and hypothalamus. He continues to state that rhythm and sequencing of sounds (dance, chants) stimulate first the temporal lobe, and onward stimulates the amygdale and the hippocampus; and that stimulation of the hippocampus may create supernatural experiences.[22]

Rhawn Joseph writes that: "The hippocampus can create a cognitive map of an individual's environment and their movements of others within."[23] "Under conditions of hyper activation (such as in response to extreme fear) it appears that the hippocampus may create a visual hallucination of that "cognitive map" such that the individual may "experience" themselves as outside their body, observing all that is occurring and/or hallucinate themselves as moving about in that environment such as flying above it."[24]

Limbic System: Hypothalamus and Pituitary Gland

Andrew Newberg, Eugene d'Aguili and Vince Rause describe that the hypothalamus is (seen from an evolutionary perspective) the oldest structure in the human limbic system, located near the upper end of the brain stem. It has an inner section (connected to the parasympathetic-quiescent nervous system), and an outer section (connected to the sympathetic-arousal nervous system). They also write that during meditation certain hormones are released which are controlled by the hypothalamus (such as vasopressin released by the posterior lobe of the pituitary gland).[25] They conclude that: "..therefore it is highly likely that something is happening in the hypothalamus during spiritual experiences and religious practice."[26]

Professor Richard A. Bowen of the Department of Biomedical Sciences, Animal Reproduction and Biotechnology Laboratory at Colorado State University states that: "The hypothalamus is a region of the brain that controls an immense number of bodily functions. It is located in the middle of the base of the brain, and encapsulates the ventral portion of the third ventricle. The pituitary gland, also known as the hypophysis, is a roundish organ that lies immediately beneath the hypothalamus (and is actually considered an extension of the hypothalamus), resting in a depression of the base of the skull called the sella turcica ("Turkish saddle"). In an adult human the pituitary is roughly the size and shape of a garbanzo bean."[27]

Diana Weedman Molavi PhD of the Washington University School of Medicine writes that: "The main function of the hypothalamus is homeostasis (through hormone secretion), or maintaining the body's status quo. Factors such as blood pressure, body temperature, fluid and electrolyte balance, and body weight are held to a precise value called the set-point. Although this set-point can migrate over time, from day to day it is remarkably fixed."[28]

Limbic System: Thalamus

The thalamus is a large egg-shaped mass of nerve cells situated in the posterior part of the forebrain that transmits sensory impulses (except smell) to the cerebral cortex (the outer layer of the brain that acts as an information network and is responsible for higher brain functions such as sensation, voluntary muscle movement, thought, reasoning, and memory).

It is considered the brain within the brain. The thalamus negotiates what state to be in, particularly when it comes to Alpha and Beta. In addition, the thalamus negotiates about the transitions between Delta and the higher states. The thalamus is a transmission center that facilitates sensory stimuli to induce corresponding physical reactions as well as affecting emotions. Together with the hypothalamus, the thalamus initiates levels of sleep and alertness (states of consciousness). It is also vital to the neural feedback system controlling brain wave rhythms.[29]

Pineal Gland

The pineal gland is <u>not</u> considered to be part of the limbic system, as it is located outside of the actual brain structure. It is located near the center of the brain, deep inside the brain, between the two hemispheres, tucked in a groove where the two rounded thalamic bodies join. The pineal gland (also called the pineal body or epiphysis) is a small endocrine gland in the brain. The pineal gland is not paired, weighs about 0.1 gram, and is responsible for the production of several neurotransmitters. The gland is close to cerebrospinal fluid channels where melatonin is secreted into directly. The gland is located directly above the colliculi (located underneath the thalamus) which are transmission stations for sights and sounds, and is surrounded by the limbic system (emotional center).

Rick Strassman writes that enzymes for converting serotonin, melatonin, or tryptamine into psychedelic compounds are found in high concentrations in the pineal gland. Seratonin

163

undergoes this "methyltransferase" (attachment of a CH_3 methylgroup) to become melatonin. By twice undergoing "methyltransferase", methylate-tryptamine becomes DMT (di-methyl-tryptamine). The pineal gland posesses the highest level of serotonin anywhere in the body.The pineal gland also makes beta-carbolines, other potentially mind altering substances. Beta-carbolines prevent the breakdown of orally taken DMT by the enzyme monoamine-oxidase (MAO). Amazonian psychedlic ayahuasca contains both plants with beta-carbolines and DMT. Strassman concludes that the pineal gland produces both DMT and beta-carbolines which magnify the effects of orally taken DMT. [30]

The production of melatonin by the pineal gland is stimulated during darkness by adrenaline and noradrenaline, and inhibited by light. Adrenaline and noradrenaline are released by nerve cells that nearly touch the pineal gland. There is a pathway from the retinas to the hypothalamus called the retinohypothalamic tract. It brings information about light and dark cycles to a region of the hypothalamus called the suprachiasmatic nucleus (SCN). From the SCN, nerve impulses travel via the pineal nerve (sympathetic nervous system) to the pineal gland. These impulses inhibit the production of melatonin. When these impulses stop (at night, when light no longer stimulates the hypothalamus), pineal inhibition ceases and melatonin is released. The pineal gland is therefore a photosensitive organ and an important timekeeper for the human body. In evolutionary older animals (lizards, amphibians) it is an actual third eye with lens, cornea and retina. In these animals it regulates body temperature and skin coloration.

Rick Strassman writes that the human pineal gland first becomes visible in the fetus at forty-nine days. This is the same moment in which male/female gender is first indicated. This coincides with the first DMT production in the gland.[31]

The pineal gland shrinks with age. It appears to play a major role in sexual development, hibernation in animals, metabolism, and seasonal breeding. Calcification of the pineal gland is typical in adults.

Elly Crystal writes: "Rene Descartes called this gland the seat of the soul. It is also referred to as the third eye ("inner vision"), or sixth chakra in eastern philosophy. The pineal gland secretes melanin during times of relaxation and visualization. In the theta brain wave state during dreaming or meditation, we are resting deeply and still conscious, at the threshold of drifting away from or back into conscious awareness. As the brain enters deeper states, our consciousness is less concerned with the physical state, our 'third eye' is active, and separation becomes natural. Many native traditions and mystical practices refer to the ability of 'seeing,' or being aware of energy fields at higher levels. This 'seeing' refers to the sight of the 'third eye'."[32]

NEUROCHEMICALS

Neurochemical: DMT

DMT (di-methyl-tryptamine) is a derivative of the amino acid tryptophan. There is a strong argument for the production of DMT within the pineal gland in minute quantities. (Lung, liver, blood and eye also possess the same raw materials for DMT production, but these organs are further removed from the ideal surroundings of the pineal in the brain).

This pineal DMT argument is as follows according to Rick Strassman: "The human pineal gland first becomes visible in the fetus at forty-nine days. This is the same moment in which male/female gender is first indicated. It takes forty-nine days for the soul to reincarnate, according to the Tibetan Buddhist Book of the Dead. This coincides with the first DMT production in the gland. In some of us, pineal DMT mediates the pivotal experiences of deep meditation, psychosis, and near-death experiences. As we die, the pineal gland releases a flood of DMT. Thus it seems that during the entering and parting of the life-force (soul) into our bodies, pineal DMT production is accelerated. Stress-induced catecholamine output (adrenaline and noradrenaline) stimulates melatonin production, and in fact may also stimulate pineal DMT production. Stress worsens hallucinations and delusions in psychotic patients. The more intense the emotion, the higher the level of DMT. Methyltransferase enzymes that form DMT are more active in schizophrenia than in normal conditions. The enzyme monoamine-oxidase MAO is less efficient in schizophrenics in destroying DMT (which may result that DMT is not cleared quickly enough from their systems). Massive doses of stress hormones also mark near-death experiences (NDE). Pineal tissue in the dying or recently dead may produce DMT for a few hours. The body defends the pineal gland against ordinary stress as to not disable us by augmenting stress-related psychedelic DMT levels. Pineal DMT production could stimulate AESC through prayer and meditation. Meditation techniques change the brain-wave frequencies to a lower vibration in a certain field (theta or lower alpha). Objects in this field vibrate in resonance, such as for example the pineal gland, which may produce more DMT. Coincidentally, the brain-wave-frequency during dreaming and meditation is similar. Melatonin production is highest during dreamtime. High stress induced by sexual activity (strenuous exertion, hyperventilation, intense emotions) may activate DMT release. Psychedelic features seem to emerge at orgasm. Tantra practitioners use a meditation of sex and meditation to achieve AESC. Both meditation and sex together may produce psychedelic effects."[1]

Neurochemical: Serotonin

Serotonin (5-HT or 5-hydroxytryptamine) is a derivative of the amino acid ryptophan. It is believed to play an important role in the central nervous system in the regulation of mood, sleep, emesis (vomiting), sexuality and appetite. Serotonin apparently also plays a part in many disorders, notably as part of the biochemistry of depression, migraine, bipolar disorder and anxiety. It may also play an important role in liver regeneration and it induces cell division throughout the body. Serotonin is also synthesized in the gastrointestinal tract in addition to the central nervous system. Too much or too little serotonin can result in imbalances.[2]

"Serotonin is synthesized in serotonergic neurons in the central nervous system and enterochromaffin cells in the gastrointestinal tract. The major storage place is platelets in the blood stream. The neurons of the Raphe nuclei are the principal source of serotonin release in the brain. The raphe nuclei are grouped into about nine pairs, distributed along the entire length of the brainstem. Seratonin carried in the bloodstream is responsible for contracting the muscles lining the veins and arteries. In the central nervous system, serotonin is believed to play an important role in the regulation of body temperature, mood, sleep, vomiting, sexuality, and appetite. Low levels of serotonin have been associated with several disorders, notably clinical depression, migraine, irritable bowel syndrome, tinnitus, fibromyalgia, bipolar disorder, and anxiety disorders."[3]

Rhawn Joseph writes that: "..serotonin restricts perceptual and information processing and in fact increases the threshold for neural responses to occur at both the neocortical and limbic levels."[4]

Neurochemical: Melatonin
Melatonin (5-methoxy-N-acetyltryptamine) is a derivative of the amino acid tryptophan.[5] Melatonin is produced within the pineal gland where serotonin is acetylated and then methylated (attaching methyl group) to yield melatonin.[6]

Strassman explains that neurotransmitters noradrenaline (norepinephrine) and adrenaline (epinephrine) – called catecholamines-, which are released by nerve cells that nearly touch the pineal gland, turn on melatonin synthesis in the pineal gland (unlike those produced at the adrenal glands which are secreted into the blood but never get to the pineal). Those catecholamines released by the adrenal glands (under for example stress) and excreted into the bloodstream do not access the pineal gland, and are instead disposed off, therefore these do not have any influence on melatonin production. However, if the stress is great enough, they do have access and augment melatonin production.[7]

Melatonin acts as an endocrine hormone since it is released into the blood, whereas melatonin produced by the retina and the gastrointestinal tract acts as a paracrine hormone (signaling agent).

The production of melatonin by the pineal gland is inhibited by light and permitted by darkness. The secretion of melatonin peaks in the middle of the night, and gradually falls during the second half of the night. Melatonin contributes to the early morning drop in body temperature, when melatonin levels are highest. The most likely time for us to dream is around this time when melatonin levels are highest.

Reduced melatonin levels turn on sexual functions, enhanced melatonin levels shrinks sexual organs (and thus has an anti-reproductive effect). The abundant melatonin levels in children is believed to inhibit sexual development. When puberty arrives, melatonin production is reduced dramatically.

Melatonin is a powerful anti-oxydant. In animal models, melatonin has been demonstrated to prevent the damage to DNA by some carcinogens, stopping the mechanism by which they cause cancer. Melatonin is an immuno-regulator that enhances T cell production somewhat.

Neurochemical: Encephalin
Encephalin (also written with a "c" instead of "k") are the smallest of the molecules with pain killing or opiate activity. They are endogenous opioids. Encephalins are found in the thalamus of the brain and in some parts of the spinal cord that transmit pain impulses. Encephalins bind to opiate receptors and release controlled levels of pain.

Dr. Manik Hirandani writes: "Endorphins and encephalins are morphine like substances, which block the ability of the brain to perceive pain."[8]

Neurochemical: Acetylcholine
Acetylcholine is released at the end of nerve fibers in ERTAS, and is involved in the transmission of nerve impulses through the body.[9] This chemical is therefore classified as a neurotransmitter. It stimulates secretion by all glands that receive parasympathetic nerve impulses (such as the locus coeruleus and raphe nuclei). It is particularly important in the stimulation of muscle tissue. The same website also lists that acetylcholine affects several of the body's systems, including the cardiovascular system (decreases heart rate and contraction strength, dilates blood vessels), gastrointestinal

system (increases peristalsis in the stomach and amplitude of digestive contractions), urinary system (decreases bladder capacity, increases voluntary voiding pressure), and respiratory system. It is important in memory and learning and is deficient in the brains of those with late-stage Alzheimer disease. One of the acetylcholine receptors is permeable to sodium and potassium ions in the brain. Thus acetylcholine is also indirectly responsible for the resetting of the sodium/potassium levels in brain cells during the theta brainwave state. One of the important tasks of sodium and potassium is the transmission of nerve impulses. After an extended period in the Beta state the ratio between potassium and sodium is out of balance and results in mental fatigue. A short period between 5-15 minutes in the Theta state restores this ratio back to normal.

PART V

NOTES, REFERENCES AND BIBLIOGRAPHY

NOTES AND REFERENCES

Introduction
1. Graham Hancock in *Supernatural: Meetings with the ancient teachers of mankind* (2005)
2. Rhawn Joseph in his chapter *Mythologies of Modern Science* in *Neurotheology: Brain, Science, Spirituality, Religious Experience* (2003) by Rhawn Joseph et al.
3. Andrew Newberg in his chapter *Bringing "Neuro" and "Theology" Together Again* in the book by Rhawn Joseph et al., in *Neurotheology: Brain, Science, Spirituality, Religious Experience* (2003:145).

Part I – Background Basics

Consciousness, The Body, and Altered States
1. Robert A. Monroe in *Far Journeys* (1985)
2. http://www.answers.com/subconsciousness
3. Rosalind A. McKnight describes in *Cosmic Journeys: My Out-of-Body Explorations with Robert A. Monroe* (1999:54)
4. idem pp.166-167
5. idem pp.57-58
6. idem pp.117
7. Robert Monroe in *Far Journeys* (1985)
8. Robert Monroe in *Ultimate Journey* (1994)

ODRs (Other Dimensions of Reality)
1. http://en.wikipedia.org/wiki/VY_Canis_Majoris
2. http://en.wikipedia.org/wiki/Quasar
3. Brian Weis in *Messages from the Masters: Tapping into the Power of Love* (2000:161)
4. idem pp.164
5. Brian Weiss in *Only Love is Real: A Story of Soulmates Reunited* ([1997] 2000:63)
6. idem pp.62
7. Rosalind A. McKnight in *Cosmic Journeys: My Out-of-Body Explorations with Robert A. Monroe* (1999:227-230)
8. Grace Davie in *Religion in Britain Since 1945: Believing without Belonging - Making Contemporary Britain* ([1994] 1995:1)

9. Robert A. Monroe in *Ultimate Journey* (1994:224-225)
10. Rosalind A. McKnight in *Cosmic Journeys: My Out-of-Body Explorations with Robert A. Monroe* (1999) (pp.226-231)
11. idem pp. 143
12. Andrew Newberg, Eugene d'Aguili and Vince Rause describe in their book *Why God won't go away: Brain Science and the Biology of Belief* (2001)
13. idem pp. 36
14. Andrew Newberg and Mark Robert Waldman write in *Why we Believe What we Believe: Uncovering Our Biological Need for Meaning, Spirituality, and Truth* (2006:55)
15. idem pp. 65
16. Matthew Alper writes in his book *The "God" Part of the Brain: A Scientific Interpretation of Human Spirituality and God* (2000:2)
17. Laurence O. McKinney states in *Neurotheology. Virtual Religion in the 21st Century* (1994:29)
18. Timothy Leary marks in *Your Brain is God* (1988:122)
19. Rosalind A. McKnight in *Cosmic Journeys: My Out-of-Body Explorations with Robert A. Monroe* (1999:204)
20. idem pp. 227-230
21. Robert A. Monroe in *Ultimate Journey* (1994)
22. Rosalind A. McKnight in *Cosmic Journeys: My Out-of-Body Explorations with Robert A. Monroe* (1999)
23. idem pp.209
24. idem pp.223
25. Rosalind A. McKnight in *Cosmic Journeys: My Out-of-Body Explorations with Robert A. Monroe* (1999)
26. Terrence McKenna in *Archaic Survival* (1991:95)
27. Brian Weiss in *Messages from the Masters: Tapping into the Power of Love* (2000:156)
28. Michael Newton in *Destiny of Souls: New Case Studies of Life between Lives* ([2000] 2005:3)
29. Sylvia Browne and Lindsay Harrison in *Life on the Other Side: A Psychic's Tour of the Afterlife* (2000:66)
30. Robert A. Monroe in *Ultimate Journey* (1994)
31. Graham Hancock in *Supernatural: Meetings with the ancient teachers of mankind* (2005).
32. Robert A. Monroe in *Far Journeys* (1985)
33. Robert A. Monroe in *Far Journeys* (1985:510)
34. idem
35. Robert A. Monroe in *Ultimate Journey* (1994)
36. Rosalind A. McKnight in *Cosmic Journeys: My Out-of-Body Explorations with Robert A. Monroe* (1999)
37. idem pp.205
38. idem pp.234-236

39. Robert A. Monroe in *Ultimate Journey* (1994:196)
40. idem pp.210
41. Rick Strassman quotes a volunteer in *DMT, The Spirit Molecule. A Doctor's Revolutionary Research into the Biology of Near-Death and Mystical Experiences* (2005:191)
42. Robert A. Monroe in *Ultimate Journey* (1994:248-249)
43. Brian Weiss in *Same Soul, Many Bodies. Discover the Healing Power of Future Lives Through Progression Therapy* (2005:11)
44. Niels Hendrik Gregersen in *Competitive Dynamics and Cultural Evolution of Religions and God Concepts* (2005)
45. Robert A. Monroe in *Ultimate Journey* (1994)
46. (pp. 249)
47. Rick Strassman's research with DMT as described in *DMT, The Spirit Molecule. A Doctor's Revolutionary Research into the Biology of Near-Death and Mystical Experiences* (2005)
48. Sylvia Browne and Lindsay Harrison describe the Ultimate Reality in *Life on the Other Side: A Psychic's Tour of the Afterlife* (2000)
49. Sylvia Browne and Lindsay Harrison describe traveling to the Ultimate Reality in *Life on the Other Side: A Psychic's Tour of the Afterlife* (2000:49)
50. idem pp. 52
51. idem pp. 54
52. Robert A. Monroe in *Ultimate Journey* (1994)
53. Brian Weiss quotes his hypnotized patient Catherine in *Many Lives, Many Masters: The True Story of a Prominent Psychiatrist, his Young Patient and the Past-Life Therapy that changed both Their Lives* (1994:83)
54. Michael Newton in *Destiny of Souls: New Case Studies of Life between Lives* ([2000] 2005:1)
55. idem pp. 306
56. Sylvia Browne and Lindsay Harrison in *Life on the Other Side: A Psychic's Tour of the Afterlife* (2000:79)
57. Sylvia Browne and Lindsay Harrison write in *Life on the Other Side: A Psychic's Tour of the Afterlife* (2000)
58. Robert A. Monroe in *Ultimate Journey* (1994)
59. Michael Newton in *Destiny of Souls: New Case Studies of Life between Lives* ([2000] 2005)
60. Sylvia Browne and Lindsay Harrison write in *Life on the Other Side: A Psychic's Tour of the Afterlife* (2000)
61. According to Michael Newton in *Destiny of Souls: New Case Studies of Life between Lives* ([2000] 2005:274)
62. Brian Weis writes in *Messages from the Masters: Tapping into the Power of Love* (2000:160-161)

63. Michael Newton in *Destiny of Souls: New Case Studies of Life between Lives* ([2000] 2005:243)

64. Sylvia Browne and Lindsay Harrison write in *Life on the Other Side: A Psychic's Tour of the Afterlife* (2000)

65. Brian Weis writes in *Messages from the Masters: Tapping into the Power of Love* (2000)

66. Michael Newton in *Destiny of Souls: New Case Studies of Life between Lives* ([2000] 2005:203)

67. Sylvia Browne and Lindsay Harrison describe the different goals and challenges of our chart in *Life on the Other Side: A Psychic's Tour of the Afterlife* (2000)

68. Michael Newton in *Destiny of Souls: New Case Studies of Life between Lives* ([2000] 2005:152)

69. idem pp. 279

70. Sylvia Browne and Lindsay Harrison refer to the place where Life Books are held as the "Hall of Records" in *Life on the Other Side: A Psychic's Tour of the Afterlife* (2000:32).

71. Rosalind A. McKnight describes in *Cosmic Journeys: My Out-of-Body Explorations with Robert A. Monroe* (1999:229)

72. Graham Hancock in *Supernatural: Meetings with the ancient teachers of mankind* (2005)

73. Brian Weiss in *Many Lives, Many Masters: The True Story of a Prominent Psychiatrist, his Young Patient and the Past-Life Therapy that changed both Their Lives* (1994:46)

74. idem pp.54

75. idem pp.68

76. idem pp.83-84

77. Brian Weiss in *Through Time into Healing. Discovering the Power of Regression Therapy to Erase Trauma and Transform Mind, Body, and Relationships* (1993:89)

78. Michael Newton in *Destiny of Souls: New Case Studies of Life between Lives* ([2000] 2005:77)

79. Sylvia Browne and Lindsay Harrison in *Life on the Other Side: A Psychic's Tour of the Afterlife* (2000:46)

80. idem pp.81-82

81. Brian Weiss quotes Catharine, his hypnotized patient, in his book *Many Lives, Many Masters: The True Story of a Prominent Psychiatrist, his Young Patient and the Past-Life Therapy that changed both Their Lives* (1994:85):

82. Brian Weis in *Messages from the Masters: Tapping into the Power of Love* (2000:61)

83. idem pp. 11

84. idem pp. 44

85. idem pp. 45

86. idem pp. 12

87. Sylvia Browne and Lindsay Harrison in *Life on the Other Side: A Psychic's Tour of the Afterlife* (2000)
88. Michael Newton in *Destiny of Souls: New Case Studies of Life between Lives* ([2000] 2005:190)
89. idem pp. 290
90. Brian Weiss in *Same Soul, Many Bodies. Discover the Healing Power of Future Lives Through Progression Therapy* (2005)
91. Michael Newton in *Destiny of Souls: New Case Studies of Life between Lives* ([2000] 2005:354)

Religion and Science

1. Timothy Leary in *Your Brain is God* (1988:25)
2. Émile Durkheim in *The Elementary Forms of the Religious Life* ([1912] 1995)
3. Rosalind A. McKnight in *Cosmic Journeys: My Out-of-Body Explorations with Robert A. Monroe* (1999:236)
4. William Arntz, Betsy Chasse and Mark Vicente in *What the Bleep do we Know: Discovering the Endless Possibilities for Altering your Everyday Reality* (2005)
5. John O.M. Bockris in *The New Paradigm: A Confrontation between Physics and The Paranormal Phenomena* (2006:233).
6. Andrew Newberg, Eugene d'Aquili and Vince Rause in *Why God Won't go Away: Brain Science & The Biology of Belief* (2001:2)
7. idem pp.108
8. idem pp.108
9. idem pp.145
10. Andrew Newberg and Mark Robert Waldman in *Why we Believe What we Believe: Uncovering Our Biological Need for Meaning, Spirituality, and Truth* (2006:87)
11. idem pp.87

The Brain

1. Andrew Newberg, Eugene d'Aguili and Vince Rause describe in their book *Why God won't go away: Brain Science and the Biology of Belief* (2001:33)
2. Rosalind A. McKnight describes in *Cosmic Journeys: My Out-of-Body Explorations with Robert A. Monroe* (1999:148)
3. idem pp.202-203
4. Carol Rausch Albright states in her chapter *Religious Experience, Complexification & the Image of God* in *Neurotheology: Brain, Science, Spirituality, Religious Experience* by Rhawn Joseph et al., (2003:180)
5. Laurence O. McKinney writes in *Neurotheology. Virtual Religion in the 21st Century* (1994)

6. Carol Raush Albright and James B. Ashbrook explain in *Where God lives in the Human Brain* (2001)

7. Andrew Newberg and Mark Robert Waldman explain in *Why we Believe What we Believe: Uncovering Our Biological Need for Meaning, Spirituality, and Truth* (2006)

8. Carol Raush Albright and James B. Ashbrook further write in *Where God lives in the Human Brain* (2001)

9. Andrew Newberg and Mark Robert Waldman concur with this notion in *Why we Believe What we Believe: Uncovering Our Biological Need for Meaning, Spirituality, and Truth* (2006).

10. Andrew Newberg, Eugene d'Aguili and Vince Rause describe in their book *Why God won't go away: Brain Science and the Biology of Belief* (2001)

11. Carol Raush Albright and James B. Ashbrook explain in *Where God lives in the Human Brain* (2001)

12. Carol Rausch Albright explains in her chapter *Religious Experience, Complexification & the Image of God* in *Neurotheology: Brain, Science, Spirituality, Religious Experience* (2003) by Rhawn Joseph et al.,

13. Catherine E. Myers in her article *Memory Loss and the Brain* (2006)
http://www.memorylossonline.com/glossary/cerebellum.html.

14. Carol Raush Albright and James B. Ashbrook explain in *Where God lives in the Human Brain* (2001)

15. idem pp.78

16. Carol Rausch Albright explains in her book chapter *Religious Experience, Complexification & the Image of God* in *Neurotheology: Brain, Science, Spirituality, Religious Experience* (2003) by Rhawn Joseph et al.

17. Carol Rausch Albright in her book chapter *Religious Experience, Complexification & the Image of God* in *Neurotheology: Brain, Science, Spirituality, Religious Experience* (2003) by Rhawn Joseph et al

18. Frazer Watts writes in his chapter *Interacting Cognitive Subsystems & Religious Meanings* in *Neurotheology: Brain, Science, Spirituality, Religious Experience* (2003) by Rhawn Joseph et al.

19. Andrew Newberg and Jeremy Iversen mentioned in their chapter *On the "Neuro" in Neurotheology* in *Neurotheology: Brain, Science, Spirituality, Religious Experience* (2003) by Rhawn Joseph et al.

20. Laurence O. McKinney writes in *Neurotheology. Virtual Religion in the 21st Century* (1994)

21. Rhawn Joseph writes in his chapter *After-Death, Astral Projection, Judgment Day & the Second Death* in *Neurotheology:*

Brain, Science, Spirituality, Religious Experience by Rhawn Joseph et al., (2003)

Part II – Travel Means & Methods and their Neurotheological Aspects

Travel Advisory
n/a

Psychedelics
1. Timothy Leary in *Your Brain is God* (1988:11)
2. Matthew Alper in *The "God" Part of the Brain. A Scientific Interpretation of Human Spirituality and God* (2000:125) that:
3. Andrew Newberg and Mark Robert Waldman in *Why we Believe What we Believe: Uncovering Our Biological Need for Meaning, Spirituality, and Truth* (2006:49)
4. idem pp. 59
5. Graham Hancock in *Supernatural: Meetings with the ancient teachers of mankind* (2005)
6. Terence McKenna in *The Archaic Revival* (1991)
7. idem pp.11
8. idem pp.17
9. Manie Eager and Enmarie Potgieter in their chapter *Exploring the Contours of Mind & Consciousness through Magico-Spiritual Techniques* in *Neurotheology: Brain, Science, Spirituality, Religious Experience* (2003) by Rhawn Joseph et al.,
10. Michael Winkelman in his chapter *Shamanism and Innate Brain Structures: The Original Neurotheology* in *Neurotheology: Brain, Science, Spirituality, Religious Experience* (2003) by Rhawn Joseph et al.,
11. Graham Hancock in *Supernatural: Meetings with the ancient teachers of mankind* (2005),
12. Terence McKenna in *The Archaic Revival* (1991)
13. Graham Hancock in *Supernatural: Meetings with the ancient teachers of mankind* (2005),
14. Rick Strassman in *DMT, the Spirit Molecule: A Doctor's Revolutionary Research into the Biology of Near-Death and Mystical Experiences* (2001)
15. Graham Hancock in *Supernatural: Meetings with the ancient teachers of mankind* (2005),
16. Rick Strassman in *DMT, the Spirit Molecule: A Doctor's Revolutionary Research into the Biology of Near-Death and Mystical Experiences* (2001: 183)
17. Terence McKenna in *The Archaic Revival* (1991)
18. idem pp.135

19. idem pp.140
20. Jeremy Narby in *The Cosmic Serpent, DNA and the Origins of Knowledge* (1999:10-11)
21. idem
22. Graham Hancock writes in *Supernatural: Meetings with the ancient teachers of mankind* (2005)
23. John O.M. Bockris in *The New Paradigm: A Confrontation between Physics and The Paranormal Phenomena* (2006:405):
24. idem pp.419
25. Timothy Leary in *Your Brain is God* (1988:52)
26. Timothy Leary in *Your Brain is God* (1988)
27. Rhawn Joseph writes in his chapter *After-Death, Astral Projection, Judgment Day & the Second Death* in *Neurotheology: Brain, Science, Spirituality, Religious Experience* (2003) by Rhawn Joseph et al.,
28. Terence McKenna in *The Archaic Revival* (1991)
29. Graham Hancock in *Supernatural: Meetings with the ancient teachers of mankind* (2005)
30. Rick Strassman in *DMT, The Spirit Molecule. A Doctor's Revolutionary Research into the Biology of Near-Death and Mystical Experiences* (2005),
31. idem

Meditation and Prayer

1. Brian Weiss in *Same Soul, Many Bodies: Discover the Healing Power of Future Lives Through Progression Therapy* (2005:167)
2. Andrew Newberg, Eugene d'Aguili and Vince Rause in *Why God won't go away: Brain Science and the Biology of Belief* (2001).
3. Brian Weiss in *Same Soul, Many Bodies: Discover the Healing Power of Future Lives Through Progression Therapy* (2005:167)
4. Rosalind A. McKnight in *Cosmic Journeys: My Out-of-Body Explorations with Robert A. Monroe* (1999:135)
5. Andrew Newberg, Eugene d'Aguili and Vince Rause in *Why God won't go away: Brain Science and the Biology of Belief* (2001)
6. idem pp.249
7. Andrew Newberg, Eugene d'Aguili and Vince Rause in *Why God won't go away: Brain Science and the Biology of Belief* (2001)
8. John O.M. Bockris in book *The New Paradigm: A Confrontation between Physics and The Paranormal Phenomena* (2006:405)
9. Andrew Newberg, Eugene d'Aguili and Vince Rause in *Why God won't go away: Brain Science and the Biology of Belief* (2001)
10. idem pp.34
11. Andrew Newberg and Mark Robert Waldman in *Why we Believe What we Believe: Uncovering Our Biological Need for Meaning, Spirituality, and Truth* (2006)

12. idem pp.214
13. Andrew Newberg, Eugene d'Aguili and Vince Rause in *Why God won't go away: Brain Science and the Biology of Belief* (2001)
14. Scott Atran in his chapter *The Neuropsychology of Religion* in the book by Rhawn Joseph et al., in *Neurotheology: Brain, Science, Spirituality, Religious Experience* (2003)
15. Andrew Newberg, Eugene d'Aguili and Vince Rause in *Why God won't go away: Brain Science and the Biology of Belief* (2001)
16. Scott Atran in his chapter *The Neuropsychology of Religion* in the book by Rhawn Joseph et al., in *Neurotheology: Brain, Science, Spirituality, Religious Experience* (2003)
17. idem pp.149
18. idem pp.149
19. Rhawn Joseph in his chapter *Dreams, Spirits and the Soul* in *Neurotheology: Brain, Science, Spirituality, Religious Experience* by Rhawn Joseph et al., (2003:411)
20. Rhawn Joseph in his chapter *Dreams, Spirits and the Soul* in *Neurotheology: Brain, Science, Spirituality, Religious Experience* by Rhawn Joseph et al., (2003)

Regression Hypnosis

1. Dr. Arthur Janov in his web-article *The Nature of* Hypnosis (2005)
   http://www.primaltherapy.com/GrandDelusions/GD02.htm
2. idem
3. idem
4. Brian Weiss in *Through Time into Healing. Discovering the Power of Regression Therapy to Erase Trauma and Transform Mind, Body, and Relationships* (1993)
5. Brian Weiss in *Many Lives, Many Masters: The True Story of a Prominent Psychiatrist, his Young Patient and the Past-Life Therapy that changed both Their Lives* (1994:24)
6. Brian Weiss in *Same Soul, Many Bodies. Discover the Healing Power of Future Lives Through Progression Therapy* (2005:22-23),
7. Brian Weiss writes in *Through Time into Healing. Discovering the Power of Regression Therapy to Erase Trauma and Transform Mind, Body, and Relationships* (1993:24-25)
8. Brian Weiss in *Same Soul, Many Bodies. Discover the Healing Power of Future Lives Through Progression Therapy* (2005:24)
9. Michael Newton in *Destiny of Souls: New Case Studies of Life between Lives* ([2000] 2005:257)
10. Michael Newton in *Destiny of Souls: New Case Studies of Life between Lives* ([2000] 2005)
11. idem pp.250

12. Sylvia Browne and Lindsay Harrison in *Past Lives, Future Healings: A Psychic Reveals the Secrets to Good Health and Great Relationships* (2002)
13. Sylvia Browne and Lindsay Harrison *Life on the Other Side: A Psychic's Tour of the Afterlife* (2000)
14. Brian Weis writes in *Messages from the Masters: Tapping into the Power of Love* (2000:186)
15. Newton in *Destiny of Souls: New Case Studies of Life between Lives* ([2000] 2005:85)
16. idem pp.79
17. Brian Weiss quotes his hypnotized patient in *Many Lives, Many Masters: The True Story of a Prominent Psychiatrist, his Young Patient and the Past-Life Therapy that changed both Their Lives* (1994:121)
18. idem pp.124
19. Newton writes in *Destiny of Souls: New Case Studies of Life between Lives* ([2000] 2005:394)
20. idem pp.24
21. idem pp.31
22. Sylvia Browne and Lindsay Harrison write in *Past Lives, Future Healings: A Psychic Reveals the Secrets to Good Health and Great Relationships* (2002)
23. Dr. Arthur Janov in his web-article *The Nature of* Hypnosis (2005)
    http://www.primaltherapy.com/GrandDelusions/GD02.htm
24. idem
25. idem
26. Anna Gossline quoting psychologist John Gruzelier in her web-article *Hypnosis really changes your* mind (2004)
    http://www.newscientist.com/article.ns?id=dn6385
27. Marie-Elisabeth Faymonville , Laurence Roediger, Guy Del Fiore, Christian Delgueldre, Christophe Phillips, Maurice Lamy, Andre Luxen, Pierre Maquet, Steven Laureys in their research paper *Increased Cerebral Functional Connectivity underlying the Antinociceptive Effects of Hypnosis* in the magazine Cognitive Brain Research, 2003, vol. 17, n°2, pp. 255-262 [8 page(s) (article)] (58 ref.)
    http://cat.inist.fr/?aModele=afficheN&cpsidt=15168174

Binaural Beat Stimulation

1. Graham Hancock in *Supernatural: Meetings with the ancient teachers of mankind* (2005)
2. Robert A. Monroe in *Far Journeys* (1985:3)
3. Robert. A. Monroe in *Journeys out of the Body* ([1971], 1977).

4. John O.M. Bockris in *The New Paradigm: A Confrontation between Physics and The Paranormal Phenomena* (2006)
5. idem pp.302
6. idem pp.303
7. Rosalind A. McKNight in *Cosmic Journeys: My Out-of-Body Explorations with Robert A. Monroe* (1999)
8. Bill Harris in *Thresholds of the Mind, Your Personal Roadmap to Success, Happiness and Contentment* (2002).
9. Article on the website of Intelegen Incorporated named *The Science of Audiobased Binaural Beat Brain Entrainment* (1995-2008)
   http://www.web-us.com/thescience.htm
10. Todd J. Masluk in *Peak and Other Exceptional Experiences during the Gateway Voyage* (1996)
11. idem
12. D. Brian Brady in *Binaural–Beat induced Theta EEG Activity and Hypnotic Susceptibility* (1997)
13. F. Holmes Atwater writes in *Inducing Altered States of Consciousness with a Binaural Beat Technology* (1997):
14. Robert A. Monroe writes in *Far Journeys* (1985)
15. idem pp.63
16. Robert A. Monroe in *Ultimate Journey* (1994)
17. F. Holmes Atwater in *Binaural Beats and the Regulation of Arousal Levels* (2001)
18. Julian Jaynes in *The Origins of Consciousness in the Breakdown of the Bicameral Mind* (1976:18)
19. Dr. Stuart W. Twemlow in the epilogue of Robert A. Monroe's *Journeys out of the Body* ([1971], 1977).
20. F. Holmes Atwater in *Inducing Altered States of Consciousness with a Binaural Beat Technology* (1997).
21. idem
22. idem
23. Dale S. Foster in *EEG and Subjective Correlates of Alpha-frequency Binaural-Beat Stimulation Combined with Alpha Biofeedback* (1990)

Repetitive and Rhythmic Stimulation

1. Article on the website of The Bradshaw Foundation called: *Eland Rock Art Paintings in San Art* (page 2 of 10). Article compiled by the Rock Art Research Institute (RARI) of the University of Witwatersrand, Johannesburg, South Africa.
   http://www.bradshawfoundation. com/rari/page2.php
2. Article on the website of The Metropolitan Museum of Art by Geoffrey Blundell called: *San Ethnography* (2000-2009). Geoffrey Blundell is affiliated with the Origins Centre, University of the

Witwatersrand, Johannesburg, South Africa
http://www.metmuseum.org/toah/hd/san/hd_san.htm
3. Graham Hancock in *Supernatural: Meetings with the ancient teachers of mankind* (2005).
4. Maarten van Hoek in his web-article *Site 12: The Trance Dance* (2003)
    http://mc2.vicnet.net.au/home/vhra/web/sapaint1b.html
5. Michael Winkelman in his chapter *Shamanism and Innate Brain Structures: The Original Neurotheology* in *Neurotheology: Brain, Science, Spirituality, Religious Experience* (2003) by Rhawn Joseph et al.,
6. Carol Raush Albright and James B. Ashbrook in *Where God lives in the Human Brain* (2001:103)
7. Andrew Newberg and Mark Robert Waldman in *Why we Believe What we Believe: Uncovering Our Biological Need for Meaning, Spirituality, and Truth* (2006)
8. idem pp.195
9. Brian Weiss in *Same Soul, Many Bodies. Discover the Healing Power of Future Lives Through Progression Therapy* (2005)
10. Andrew Newberg, Eugene d'Aguili and Vince Rause write in their book *Why God won't go away: Brain Science and the Biology of Belief* (2001)
11. idem pp.89
12. Carol Raush Albright and James B. Ashbrook in *Where God lives in the Human Brain* (2001)
13. Michael Winkelman in his chapter *Shamanism and Innate Brain Structures: The Original Neurotheology Neurotheology: Brain, Science, Spirituality, Religious Experience* by Rhawn Joseph et al.
14. idem pp.389
15. idem pp.390
16. Andrew Newberg, Eugene d'Aguili and Vince Rause write in *Why God won't go away: Brain Science and the Biology of Belief* (2001:79)
17. Scott Atran in his chapter *The Neuropsychology of Religion* in the book by Rhawn Joseph et al., in *Neurotheology: Brain, Science, Spirituality, Religious Experience* (2003)
18. Andrew Newberg and Mark Robert Waldman write that *Why we Believe What we Believe: Uncovering Our Biological Need for Meaning, Spirituality, and Truth* (2006)
19. idem
20. idem
21. idem
22. idem

Electric and Electro-Magnetic Stimulation

1. Graham Hancock in *Supernatural: Meetings with the ancient teachers of mankind* (2005)
2. Raymond F. Paloutzian, Thomas G. Fikes and Dirk Hutsebraut in their chapter *A Social Cognition Interpretation of Neurotheological Events* in *Neurotheology: Brain, Science, Spirituality, Religious Experience* by Rhawn Joseph et al., (2003).
3. Article on the website of the Tesla Memorial Society of New York called *A Short History of the Magnetic Resonance Imaging (MRI)* http://teslasociety.com/mri.htm
4. Michael A. Persinger in his chapter *Experimental Simulation of the God Experience* in *Neurotheology: Brain, Science, Spirituality, Religious Experience* by Rhawn Joseph et al., (2003:286)
5. idem pp.286-287
6. idem pp.279
7. Article on the website of the magazine Wired by Jack Hitt called *This is Your Brain on God* (issue 7.11, November 1999) http://www.wired.com/wired/archive/7.11/persinger.html
8. John O.M. Bockris in *The New Paradigm: A Confrontation between Physics and The Paranormal Phenomena* (2006:405)
9. idem pp.405
10. Andrew Newberg, Eugene d'Aguili and Vince Rause in *Why God won't go away: Brain Science and the Biology of Belief* (2001:42-43)
11. Raymond F. Paloutzian, Thomas G. Fikes and Dirk Hutsebraut in their chapter *A Social Cognition Interpretation of Neurotheological Events* in *Neurotheology: Brain, Science, Spirituality, Religious Experience* by Rhawn Joseph et al., (2003)
12. Laurence O. McKinney in *Neurotheology. Virtual Religion in the 21st Century* (1994)
13. idem pp.127
14. idem pp.127
15. Rhawn Joseph lists in his chapter *After-Death, Astral Projection, Judgement Day & the Second Death* in *Neurotheology: Brain, Science, Spirituality, Religious Experience* (2003) by Rhawn Joseph et al.,
16. idem pp.365
17. idem pp.365
18. Rhawn Joseph in his chapter *Sex, Violence & Religious Experience* in *Neurotheology: Brain, Science, Spirituality, Religious Experience* by Rhawn Joseph et al., (2003:475)
19. idem pp. 496
20. Rhawn Joseph writes in his chapter *After–Death, Astral Projection, Judgement Day & the Second Death* in *Neurotheology: Brain, Science, Spirituality, Religious Experience* by Rhawn

Joseph et al., (2003:382)

21. Olaf Blanke, S. Ortigue, T. Landis and M. Seeck in *Stimulating illusory own-body perceptions* in the magazine *Nature*, 2002, issue 419, pp.269-270
22. United Press' web-article *Brain stimulation creates shadow person* (2006) http://www.physorg.com/news77992285.html
23. Todd Murphey in his web-article *Neuromeditation: Neurologically-Based Spiritual Practices* (1999) http://www.shaktitechnology.com/neuromed.htm
24. Rhawn Joseph writes in his chapter *Dreams, Spirits and the Soul* in *Neurotheology: Brain, Science, Spirituality, Religious Experience* by Rhawn Joseph et al., (2003:411)
25. Rhawn Joseph writes in his chapter *Possession & Prophecy* in *Neurotheology: Brain, Science, Spirituality, Religious Experience* by Rhawn Joseph et al., (2003:554)
26. idem pp.554

Other Means to Travel

1. Scott Atran writes in his chapter *The Neuropsychology of Religion* in the book by Rhawn Joseph et al., in *Neurotheology: Brain, Science, Spirituality, Religious Experience* (2003)
2. Melissa K. Spearing, M.H.S., David Shore, M.D. and John K. Hsiao, M.D. in the booklet *Overview of Schizophrenia* NIH Publication No. 02-3517 Printed 1999, Reprinted 2002 – National Institute of Mental Health (NIMH) – also found at http://www.schizophrenia.com/family/sz.overview.htm
3. idem
4. Steven C. Schachter, M.D. in his web-article *What Causes Epilepsy* – Last Reviewed:12/15/06 http://www.epilepsy.com/101/ep101_cause.html
5. Aliyah Baruchin's article *Epilepsy's debilitating toll – and stigma* published in the International Herald Tribune (22 Feb 2007).
6. Jamie Talan in *Religion: is it all in your Head?* (1998)
7. Matthew Alper explains in *The "God" Part of the Brain. A Scientific Interpretation of Human Spirituality and God* (2000)
8. John O.M. Bockris in his book *The New Paradigm: A Confrontation between Physics and The Paranormal Phenomena* (2006:229)
9. idem pp.405
10. Rhawn Joseph in his chapter *After-Death, Astral Projection, Judgment Day & the Second Death* in *Neurotheology: Brain, Science, Spirituality, Religious Experience* (2003) by Rhawn Joseph et al.,
11. Scott Atran explains in his chapter *The Neuropsychology of Religion* in the book by Rhawn Joseph et al., in *Neurotheology:*

Brain, Science, Spirituality, Religious Experience (2003)

12. Rhawn Joseph in his chapter *Possession & Prophecy* in *Neurotheology: Brain, Science, Spirituality, Religious Experience* by Rhawn Joseph et al. (2003:532-533)

13. Matthew Alper in *The "God" Part of the Brain. A Scientific Interpretation of Human Spirituality and God* (2000).

14. Andrew Newberg, Eugene d'Aguili and Vince Rause describe in *Why God won't go away: Brain Science and the Biology of Belief* (2001)

15. idem pp.111

16. Rosalind A. McKnight in *Cosmic Journeys: My Out-of-Body Explorations with Robert A. Monroe* (1999:37)

17. Matthew Alper in *The "God" Part of the Brain. A Scientific Interpretation of Human Spirituality and God* (2000)

18. Laurence O. McKinney in *Neurotheology. Virtual Religion in the 21st Century* (1994)

19. Michael A. Persinger in his chapter *Experimental Simulation of the God Experience* in *Neurotheology: Brain, Science, Spirituality, Religious Experience* by Rhawn Joseph et al., (2003)

20. Raymond F. Paloutzian, Thomas G. Fikes and Dirk Hutsebraut in their book chapter *A Social Cognition Interpretation of Neurotheological Events* in *Neurotheology: Brain, Science, Spirituality, Religious Experience* by Rhawn Joseph et al., (2003).

21. Persinger In *Experimental Simulation of the God Experience* in *Neurotheology: Brain, Science, Spirituality, Religious Experience* by Rhawn Joseph et al., (2003:286-287)

22. John O.M. Bockris writes in his book *The New Paradigm: A Confrontation between Physics and The Paranormal Phenomena* (2006:403)

23. John O.M. Bockris writes in his book *The New Paradigm: A Confrontation between Physics and The Paranormal Phenomena* (2006)

24. Architect Stéphane Cardinaux writes in *Géométries Sacrées, Tome 2* (2006

25. Rosalind A. McKnight describes in *Cosmic Journeys: My Out-of-Body Explorations with Robert A. Monroe* (1999)

26. Graham Hancock in *Supernatural: Meetings with the ancient teachers of mankind* (2005)

27. idem pp.408

28. idem pp.493

29. Graham Hancock writes in *Supernatural: Meetings with the ancient teachers of mankind* (2005)

30. idem

31. Rick Strassman in *DMT, the Spirit Molecule: A Doctor's Revolutionary Research into the Biology of Near-Death and*

Mystical Experiences (2001)

Part III – Recapitulation

Travel Sequencing
n/a

Traveling and Vibrational Levels
1. Graham Hancock in *Supernatural: Meetings with the ancient teachers of mankind* (2005: 480)
2. Rick Strassman in *DMT. The Spirit Molecule. A Doctor's Revolutionary Research into the Biology of Near-Death and Mystical Experiences* (2005)
3. idem pp.210
4. idem pp: 231
5. idem pp. 232
6. Doctor Rick Strassman concludes in *DMT. The Spirit Molecule. A Doctor's Revolutionary Research into the Biology of Near-Death and Mystical Experiences* (2001: 315/316)
7. idem pp.327
8. Graham Hancock in *Supernatural: Meetings with the ancient teachers of mankind* (2005: 356),
9. Rhawn Joseph in his chapter *Dreams, Spirits and the Soul* in *Neurotheology: Brain, Science, Spirituality, Religious Experience* by Rhawn Joseph et al., (2003:425)
10. idem pp.413

Traveling and Neural Functions
1. R.Joseph in his chapter *Mythologies of Modern Science* in *Neurotheology: Brain, Science, Spirituality, Religious Experience* by Rhawn Joseph et al., (2003:9)
2. Rhawn Joseph in his chapter *Dreams, Spirits and the Soul* in *Neurotheology: Brain, Science, Spirituality, Religious Experience* by Rhawn Joseph et al., (2003)
3. Rhawn Joseph in his chapter *After-Death, Astral Projection, Judgement Day & the Second Death* in *Neurotheology: Brain, Science, Spirituality, Religious Experience* by Rhawn Joseph et al., (2003:385)
4. Kelly Bulkeley writes in her chapter *The Study of "Big Dreams"* in *Neurotheology: Brain, Science, Spirituality, Religious Experience* by Rhawn Joseph et al., (2003:442)
5. Michael A. Persinger in his chapter *The Temporal Lobe: The Biological Basis of the God Experience* in *Neurotheology: Brain, Science, Spirituality, Religious Experience* by Rhawn Joseph et al., (2003:274)

Traveling and Current Laws
n/a

Neurotheology and Future Research
1. Rick Strassman in *DMT, the Spirit Molecule: A Doctor's Revolutionary Research into the Biology of Near-Death and Mystical Experiences* (2001: 200):
2. Andrew Newberg, Eugene d'Aguili and Vince Rause in *Why God won't go away: Brain Science and the Biology of Belief* (2001:126)
3. idem pp.140-141
4. Graham Hancock in *Supernatural: Meetings with the ancient teachers of mankind* (2005:405)
5. idem pp.407
6. idem pp.345
7. Terence McKenna in *The Archaic Revival* (1991:69)

Part IV – Appendices

Brain Stem
1. D. Brian Brady in Binaural-Beat induced Theta EEG Activity and Hypnotic Susceptibility (1997)
2. Poul-Erik Paulev, M.D., D.Sci in *Medical Physiology and Pathophysiology, Essentials and Clinical Problems* (1999/2000). Chapter 4 "Brain Function, Locomotion and Disorder". http://www.mfi.ku.dk/ppaulev/chapter4/chapr_4.htm
3. Website of the Monroe Institute http://www.monroeinstitute.com
4. According to D. Brian Brady in *Binaural-Beat induced Theta EEG Activity and Hypnotic Susceptibility* (1997)
5. F. Holmes Atwater's in his document *Binaural Beats and the Regulation of Arousal Levels* (2001).
6. F. Holmes Atwater quotes from research performed by Empson in 1986 in *Inducing Altered States of Consciousness with a Binaural Beat Technology* (1997)

Limbic System
1. http://www.answers.com/topic/amygdala
2. Andrew Newberg and Mark Robert Waldman in *Why we Believe What we Believe: Uncovering Our Biological Need for Meaning, Spirituality, and Truth* (2006)
3. idem pp.31
4. Catherine E. Myers in her article *Memory Loss and the Brain* (2006) http://www.memorylossonline.com/glossary/amygdala.html

5. Carol Raush Albright and James B. Ashbrook in *Where God lives in th e Human Brain* (2001)
6. Andrew Newberg, Eugene d'Aguili and Vince Rause write in their book *Why God won't go away: Brain Science and the Biology of Belief* (2001)
7. Rhawn Joseph outlines in his chapter *Paleolithic Spiritual Evolution* in *Neurotheology: Brain, Science, Spirituality, Religious Experience* by Rhawn Joseph et al., (2003)
8. idem pp.343
9. Rhawn Joseph points out in his chapter *Dreams, Spirits and the Soul* in *Neurotheology: Brain, Science, Spirituality, Religious Experience* by Rhawn Joseph et al., (2003)
10. idem pp.411
11. http://www.answers.com/hippocampus
12. Carol Raush Albright and James B. Ashbrook in *Where God lives in the Human Brain* (2001)
13. Laurence O. McKinney in *Neurotheology. Virtual Religion in the 21st Century* (1994)
14. Andrew Newberg and Mark Robert Waldman in *Why we Believe What we Believe: Uncovering Our Biological Need for Meaning, Spirituality, and Truth* (2006)
15. Catherine E. Myers in her web-article *Memory Loss and the Brain* (2006)
    http://www.memorylossonline.com/glossary/hippocampus.html
16. idem
17. Poul-Erik Paulev, M.D., D.Sci in his web-article *Medical Physiology And Pathophysiology, Essentials and clinical problems* (1999/2000). Chapter 4 "Brain Function, Locomotion and Disorder".
    http://www.mfi.ku.dk/ppaulev/chapter4/chapr_4.htm
18. Rhawn Joseph quoting Gloor in his chapter *Paleolithic Spiritual Evolution* in *Neurotheology: Brain, Science, Spirituality, Religious Experience* by Rhawn Joseph et al., (2003).
19. Andrew Newberg, Eugene d'Aguili and Vince Rause in *Why God won't go away: Brain Science and the Biology of Belief* (2001)
20. idem pp.46
21. Catherine E. Myers in her web-article *Memory Loss and the Brain* (2006)
    http://www.memorylossonline.com/glossary/hippocampus.html
22. Scott Atran in his chapter *The Neuropscholigy of Religion* in the book by Rhawn Joseph et al., in *Neurotheology: Brain, Science, Spirituality, Religious Experience* (2003)
23. Rhawn Joseph in his chapter *After-Death, Astral Projection, Judgment Day & the Second Death* in *Neurotheology: Brain,*

Science, Spirituality, Religious Experience by Rhawn Joseph et al., (2003:382)

24. idem
25. Andrew Newberg, Eugene d'Aguili and Vince Rause describe in their book *Why God won't go away: Brain Science and the Biology of Belief* (2001)
26. idem pp.44
27. R.A.Bowen in his web-article *Functional Anatomy of the Hypothalamus* and *Pituitary gland* (2001)
    http://www.vivo.colostate.edu/hbooks/pathphys/endocrine/hyp opit/anatomy.html
28. Diana Weedman Molavi, PhD in her web-article *Hypothalamus and Autonomic Nervous System* (1997)
    http://thalamus.wustl.edu/course/hypoANS.html
29. The Biocybernaut Institute's web-article *Alpha Waves - Alpha Brain Waves* (2005)
    http://www.biocybernaut.com/about/brainwaves/alpha.htm
30. Rick Strassman writes in *DMT, the Spirit Molecule: A Doctor's Revolutionary Research into the Biology of Near-Death and Mystical Experiences* (2001)
31. idem
32. Elly Crystal in her web-article *Third Eye – Pineal Gland* (2009)
    http://www.crystalinks.com/thirdeyepineal.html

Neurochemicals
1. Rick Strassman in *DMT, the Spirit Molecule: A Doctor's Revolutionary Research into the Biology of Near-Death and Mystical Experiences* (2001: 68-80)
2. http://en.wikipedia.org/wiki/Serotonin
3. idem
4. Rhawn Joseph writes in his chapter *After-Death, Astral Projection, Judgment Day & the Second Death* in *Neurotheology: Brain, Science, Spirituality, Religious Experience* by Rhawn Joseph et al., (2003:365)
5. Rick Strassman's *DMT, the Spirit Molecule: A Doctor's Revolutionary Research into the Biology of Near-Death and Mystical Experiences* (2001).
6. http://en.wikipedia.org/wiki/Melatonin
7. Rick Strassman's *DMT, the Spirit Molecule: A Doctor's Revolutionary Research into the Biology of Near-Death and Mystical Experiences* (2001).
8. Dr. Manik Hiranandani in his web-article *The Scientific Basis of Acupuncture* (2009) http://www.drmanik.com/chap3.htm
9. http://www.answers.com/Acetylcholine

Part V – Notes, References and Bibliography

Images and Figures

- Cover Image "Angel Flight" by Sha'nah combined with artwork from ERICKH. "Angel Flight" reprinted with permission from Sha'nah, www.shanah.net

- Part II Travel Methods, Chapter 6 Repetitive & Rhythmic Stimulation
  Image "One Body when the Brain says Two"
  Reprinted with permission from The New York Times and Graham Roberts

- All other drawings by ERICKH
  Reprinted with permission from ERICKH, www.erickh.com

List of Tables

Table 1: Consciousness States
By Author, with the exception of:
a : Rosalind A. McKnight in *Cosmic Journeys: My Out-of-Body Explorations with Robert A. Monroe* (1999:45)
b: idem
c: idem pp.169
d: idem pp.45 and pp.170

Table 2: The Divine
From "Judaism to Zoroastrianism" compiled by author from information listed on http://en.wikipedia.org/wiki/God
"Other words for God" compiled from works listed in bibliography

Table 3: Earth and ODRs
Compiled from various works listed in bibliography.

Table 4: Brainwave States
Compiled from various works listed in bibliography.

Table 5: Psychedelics overview
Compiled from various works listed in bibliography.

Table 6: Brain scanning methods
Compiled from Andrew Newberg and Jeremy Iversen's chapter *On the "Neuro" in Neurotheology* in the book by Rhawn Joseph et al., in *Neurotheology: Brain, Science, Spirituality, Religious Experience* (2003)

Table 7: Brain activity during mystical states
Compiled from Andrew Newberg and Eugene d'Aguili's chapter *The Neuropsychology of Aesthetic, Spiritual & Mystical States* in the book by Rhawn Joseph in *Neurotheology: Brain, Science, Spirituality, Religious Experience* (2003:246) and Andrew Newberg and Mark Robert Waldman in *Why we Believe What we Believe: Uncovering Our Biological Need for Meaning, Spirituality, and Truth* (2006:178-179)

Table 8: Active "western" meditation
Compiled from the book *Why God won't go away: Brain Science and the Biology of Belief* (2001) by Andrew Newberg, Eugene d'Aguili and Vince Rause.

Table 9: Passive "eastern" meditation
Compiled from the book *Why God won't go away: Brain Science and the Biology of Belief* (2001) by Andrew Newberg, Eugene d'Aguili and Vince Rause.

Table 10: Neural lobe functions during a Pure Consciousness State due to Meditation
Compiled from chapter *The Neuropsychology of Religion* in the book by Rhawn Joseph et al., in *Neurotheology: Brain, Science, Spirituality, Religious Experience* (2003) by Scott Atran.

Table 11: Neural functions during non-AESC or normal situation
Compiled from various works listed in bibliography.

Table 12: Neural functions during AESC due to meditation
Compiled from various works listed in bibliography.

Table 13: Neural functions during a Pure Consciousness State due to prayer
Compiled from various works listed in bibliography.

Table 14: Neurochemical changes during meditation and related spiritual practices
Compiled from Andrew Newberg and Jeremy Iversen's chapter *On the "Neuro" in Neurotheology* in the book by Rhawn Joseph et al., in *Neurotheology: Brain, Science, Spirituality, Religious Experience* (2003:254-257).

Table 15: Consciousness and binaural beats
Compiled from F. Holmes Atwater in *Inducing Altered States of Consciousness with a Binaural Beat Technology* (1997).

Table 16: Neural functions during AESC due to physical repetitious movement
Compiled from various works listed in bibliography.

Table 17: Neural functions during AESC due to exhaustive physical repetitious movement combined with ongoing rhythm
Compiled from various works listed in bibliography.

Table 18: Tesla, unit of magnetic flux density
Some of the information obtained from
http://www.coolmagnetman.com/magflux.htm

Table 19: Hallucinations versus Pure consciousness states
Compiled from *Why God won't go away: Brain Science and the Biology of Belief* (2001) by Andrew Newberg, Eugene d'Aguili and Vince Rause.

Table 20: Travel method and means of AESC induction
Compiled from various works listed in bibliography.

Table 21: Brain Function, Activity and Related Feelings during different methods of obtaining AESC, and during activation of either the left or right hemisphere.
Compiled from various works listed in bibliography.

Table 22: Neurochemical activity during different methods of obtaining AESC and other states of mind.
Compiled from various works listed in bibliography.

BIBLIOGRAPHY

ALBRIGHT, Carol Rausch and ASHBROOK, James B. 2001
Where God lives in the Human Brain.
Naperville, Illinois: Sourcebooks, Inc.

ALPER, Matthew 2000
The "God" Part of the Brain. A Scientific Interpretation of Human Spirituality and God.
New York: Rogue Press.

ARNTZ, William and CHASSE, Betsy and VICENTE, Mark 2005
What the Bleep do we know?
Deerfield Beach, Florida: Health Communications Inc.

ATWATER, Holmes, F. 1997
"Inducing Altered States of Consciousness with a Binaural Beat Technology".
JOURNAL OF SCIENTIFIC EXPLORATION
Vol 11: No.3 pp. 263-274

ATWATER, Holmes, F. 2001
Binaural Beats and the Regulation of Arousal Levels.
Abstract from document published in Proceedings of the IANS 11th Forum on New Arts and Science.

BARUCHIN, Aliyah, 2007
"Epilepsy's debilitating toll – and stigma".
INTERNATIONAL HERALD TRIBUNE, February 22, pp. 10

BLANKE, O., ORTIQUE, S., LANDIS, T. and SEECK, M. 2002
"Stimulating Illusory Own-body Perceptions"
NATURE
Volume 419: pp.269-270

BLUNDELL, Geoffrey 2000-2009
Article on the website of The Metropolitan Museum of Art called: *San Ethnography*
http://www.metmuseum.org/toah/hd/san/hd_san.htm

BOCKRIS, John O.M. 2006
The New Paradigm. A Confrontation between Physics and The Paranormal Phenomena.
Normangee, Texas: D&M Enterprises Publisher.

BOWEN, R.A. 2001
Functional Anatomy of the Hypothalamus and *Pituitary gland*
http://www.vivo.colostate.edu/hbooks/pathphys/endocrine/hypopit/anatomy.html

BRADY, D. Brian 1997
Binaural-Beat induced Theta EEG Activity and Hypnotic Susceptibility. Research conducted at the Northern Arizona University: May.

BROWNE, Sylvia and HARRISON, Lindsay 2000
Life on The Other Side. A Psychic's Tour of the Afterlife.
London: Piatkus Books Ltd.

BROWNE, Sylvia and HARRISON, Lindsay 2002
Past Lives, Future Healings: A Psychic Reveals the Secrets to Good Health and Great Relationships.
London: Penguin Books Ltd.

CARDINAUX, Stéphane 2006
Géométries Sacrées, Tome 2
Paris, France: Éditions Trajectoire

DAVIE, Grace [1994] 1995
Religion in Britain Since 1945
Oxford, UK: Blackwell Publishers

DURKHEIM, Émile [1912] 1995
The Elementary Forms of the Religious Life
New York: The Free Press

FAYMONVILLE Marie-Elisabeth; ROEDIGER Laurence ; DEL FIORE Guy; DELGUELDRE Christian; PHILLIPS Christophe; LAMY Maurice; LUXEN Andre; MAQUET Pierre; LAUREYS Steven 2003
"Increased Cerebral Functional Connectivity underlying the Antinociceptive Effects of Hypnosis"
COGNITIVE BRAIN RESEARCH
vol. 17, n°2, pp. 255-262
http://cat.inist.fr/?aModele=afficheN&cpsidt=15168174

FOSTER, Dale S. 1990
EEG and Subjective Correlates of Alpha-Frequency Binaural-Beat Stimulation Combined with Alpha Biofeedback.
Independent research conducted at Memphis State University, Memphis, Tennessee

HANCOCK, Graham 2005
Supernatural. Meetings with the ancient teachers of mankind.
London, UK: Arrow Books.

HARRIS, Bill 2002
Thresholds of the Mind: Your Personal Roadmap to Success, Happiness, and Contentment.
Beaverton: Centerpointe Press.

HITT, Jack 1999
"This is Your Brain on God".
WIRED MAGAZINE
Issue 7.11, November

JANOV, Arthur Janov 2005
The Nature of Hypnosis
http://www.primaltherapy.com/GrandDelusions/GD02.htm

JAYNES, Julian 1976
The Origin of Consciousness in the Breakdown of the Bicameral Mind.
Boston: Houghton Mifflin Company

JOSEPH, Rhawn et al. 2002
Neurotheology. Brain, Science, Spirituality, Religious Experience.
San Jose, California: University Press California.

GREGERSEN, Niels Hendrik 2005
Field Analysis for a New Research Initiative on: *Competitive Dynamics and Cultural Evolution of Religions and God Concepts.*
Prepared for the Metanexus Institute on Religion and Science and the John Templeton Foundation.

GOSSLINE, Anna 2004
Hypnosis really changes your mind
http://www.newscientist.com/article.ns?id=dn6385

HIRANANDANI, Manik 2009
The Scientific Basis of Acupuncture
http://www.drmanik.com/chap3.htm

LANBO, Jeff 2001
"Wired for Sound".
AUDITORY/VISUAL STIMULATION Vol. 1 (Winter, #2): pages 6-10

LEARY, Timothy 1988
Your Brain is God.
Berkeley, California: Ronin Publishing, Inc.

PAULEY, Poul-Erik Paulev 1999-2000
Medical Physiology And Pathophysiology, Essentials and clinical problems
Chapter 4 "Brain Function, Locomotion and Disorder"
Copenhagen: Copenhagen Medical Publishers

MASLUK, Todd J. 1996
Peak and Other Exceptional Experiences during the Gateway Voyage.
Research conducted on behalf of the Monroe Institute.

MCKENNA, Terrence 1991
The Archaic Revival
New York, New York: HarperCollins Publishers.

MCKINNEY, Laurence O. 1994
Neurotheology. Virtual Religion in the 21st Century.
Cambridge, MA: American Institute for Mindfulness.

MCKNIGHT, Rosalind A. 1999
Cosmic Journeys: My Out-of-Body Explorations with Robert A. Monroe.
Charlottesville: Hampton Roads Publishing Company.

MYERS, Catherine E. 2006
Memory Loss and the Brain
http://www.memorylossonline.com/glossary/amygdala.html

MONROE, Robert A. [1971] 1977
Journeys out of the Body.
New York: Broadway Books

MONROE, Robert A. 1985
Far Journeys.
New York: Broadway Books

MONROE, Robert A. 1994
Ultimate Journey.
New York: Broadway Books

NARBY, Jeremy Narby [1998] 1999
The Cosmic Serpent, DNA and the Origins of Knowledge
New York: Jeremy P. Tarcher / Putnam

NEWBERG, Andrew and D'AQUILI, Eugene and RAUSE, Vince 2001
Why God won't go away. Brain Science and the Biology of Belief.
New York: Ballantine Books

NEWBERG, Andrew and WALDMAN, Mark Robert, 2006
Why We Believe What We Believe: Uncovering Our Biological Need for Meaning, Spirituality, and Truth.
New York: Free Press.

NEWTON, Michael [1994] 2005
Journey of Souls. Case Studies of Life between Lives.
St. Paul, MN: Llewellyn Publications.

NEWTON, Michael [2000] 2005
Destiny of Souls. New Case Studies of Life between Lives.
St. Paul, MN: Llewellyn Publications.
NEWTON, Michael [2004] 2005
Life between Lives. Hypnotherapy for Spiritual Regression.
St. Paul, MN: Llewellyn Publications.

SCHACHTER, Steven C. 2006
What Causes Epilepsy
http://www.epilepsy.com/101/ep101_cause.html

SLOAN WILSON, David 2005
Field Analysis for a New Research Initiative on: *Competitive Dynamics and Cultural Evolution of Religions and God Concepts.*
Prepared for the Metanexus Institute on Religion and Science and the John Templeton Foundation.

SPEARING Melissa K. and SHORE David and HSIAO John K. [1999] 2002
Overview of Schizophrenia
NIH Publication No. 02-3517
National Institute of Mental Health (NIMH)
http://www.schizophrenia.com/family/sz.overview.htm

STRASSMAN, Rick 2001
DMT. The Spirit Molecule. A Doctor's Revolutionary Research into the Biology of Near-Death and Mystical Experiences.
Rochester, Vermont: Park Street Press.

TALAN, Jamie 1998
Religion: is it all in your head?
Psychology Today
Issue March/April

VAN HOEK, Maarten van Hoek 2003
Site 12: The Trance Dance
http://mc2.vicnet.net.au/home/vhra/web/sapaint1b.html

WEEDMAN MOLAVI, Diana 1997
Hypothalamus and Autonomic Nervous System
http://thalamus.wustl.edu/course/hypoANS.html

WEISS, Brian [1988] 1994
Many lives, Many masters. The true story of a prominent psychiatrist, his young patient and the past-life therapy that changed both their lives.
London: Piatkus Books Ltd.

WEISS, Brian 1993
Through Time into Healing. Discovering the Power of Regression Therapy to Erase Trauma and Transform Mind, Body, and Relationships.
New York: Fire Side.

WEISS, Brian [1997] 2000
Only Love is Real: A Story of Soulmates Reunited.
New York: Time Warner Book Group

WEISS, Brian 2000
Messages from the Masters: Tapping into the Power of Love.
London: Piatkus Books Ltd.

WEISS, Brian 2005
Same Soul, Many Bodies. Discover the Healing Power of Future Lives Through Progression Therapy.
New York: Free Press.

Internet Resources
http://cat.inist.fr/?aModele=afficheN&cpsidt=15168174
http://en.wikipedia.org/wiki/God
http://en.wikipedia.org/wiki/Melatonin
http://en.wikipedia.org/wiki/Serotonin
http://en.wikipedia.org/wiki/Quasar
http://en.wikipedia.org/wiki/VY_Canis_Majoris

http://mc2.vicnet.net.au/home/vhra/web/sapaint1b.html
http://teslasociety.com/mri.htm
http://thalamus.wustl.edu/course/hypoANS.html
http://www.answers.com/Acetylcholine
http://www.answers.com/topic/amygdala
http://www.answers.com/hippocampus
http://www.answers.com/subconsciousness
http://www.bradshawfoundation.com/rari/page2.php
http://www.biocybernaut.com/about/brainwaves/alpha.htm
http://www.coolmagnetman.com/magflux.htm
http://www.crystalinks.com/thirdeyepineal.html
http://www.drmanik.com/chap3.htm
http://www.epilepsy.com/101/ep101_cause.html
http://www.metmuseum.org/toah/hd/san/hd_san.htm
http://www.memorylossonline.com/glossary/amygdala.html
http://www.memorylossonline.com/glossary/cerebellum.html
http://www.memorylossonline.com/glossary/hippocampus.html
http://www.mfi.ku.dk/ppaulev/chapter4/chapr_4.htm
http://www.monroeinstitute.com
http://www.newscientist.com/article.ns?id=dn6385
http://www.physorg.com/news77992285.html
http://www.primaltherapy.com/GrandDelusions/GD02.htm
http://www.schizophrenia.com/family/sz.overview.htm
http://www.shaktitechnology.com/neuromed.htm
http://www.vivo.colostate.edu/hbooks/pathphys/endocrine/hypopit/anatomy.html
http://www.web-us.com/thescience.htm
http://www.wired.com/wired/archive/7.11/persinger.html